First Edition: October 2019
Printed in the United States of America
ISBN: 13:978-1983565663
ISBN: 10: 1983565660

DEDICATION

Port Norris Historical Society

All proceeds from the sale of this book will be donated to the Port Norris Historical Society. It gives me great pleasure to help, in this small way, to support and preserve the history and memories of the town I grew up in as a boy.

Keep up the good work!

Table of Contents

Acknowledgement

I wish to thank the following people and organizations for their contributions to this book.

The Cumberland County Historical Society's Lummis Library

Greenwich, New Jersey

Olin McConnell

Cover Art

Port Norris Methodist Church

William "Bill" Saunderlin

For his willingness to always find the information needed

Kelly McCormick

Without whose help this book would not have been possible

Preface

Port Norris is located along the beginnings of the Maurice River and bordered by the Delaware Bay. Port Norris, in 1883, was divided into two sections, Port Norris, which included the town's center and North Port Norris, also known as Middletown, located from approximately where Parson's Lane intersects North Avenue to Sockwell Lane. It was given the name of Middletown because it was located between Port Norris and Haleyville. Later it became known only as North Port Norris and eventually just Port Norris as it is known today. In 1883, there were 885 people who called, Port Norris and North Port Norris, their home.

In just two short years both had experienced an explosion of growth. Houses were being built at an incredible rate and the builders could not keep up with the demand of people looking for places to live. The population had more than doubled and the oyster industry employed over 5,000 men and over 140 boats plied the waters of the Maurice River Cove and Delaware Bay, planting and harvesting that delicious, succulent oyster.

Port Norris was given the nickname of the "Oyster City" and its fortunes would rise and fall each year on the fate of the oyster. The wealth being created by this tiny mollusk was unbelievable. There were more millionaires per square mile in Port Norris than any other place in New Jersey. Port Norris, in a few short years, and for many years to come, would boast, and rightly so, of being the "Oyster Capital of the World."

This book contains information provided from newspapers of the day published in Bridgeton, New Jersey. Some people of the town, called "local correspondents" would write down the "happenings" of the week and send it to the papers to be published. The correspondents would go by nicknames or just an initial located at the end of the day's story. Hopefully, this will give us a glimpse of what life was like in our small village many years ago.

This book is the fourth in a planned series of books dedicated to our unique little oyster village, which would explode in growth and prosperity and capture the attention of an entire State.

January 5

Mr. Harry Bowden is suffering with rheumatism.

Miss Maggie Tribbett is the guest of George Reed.

Mrs. John Owens is very low.

Miss Hattie Bloxsom and Miss Carrie Bateman are putting in the holidays at home.

Edward Willis killed two fine porkers for Robert H. Bloxsman the other day.

Some Mauricetown sportsmen went gunning after rabbits. Their dogs treed something and they shot up in the tree and down came a young alligator. He had been eating peanuts. At least so saith our boss muskratter.

Several young men had a shooting match the other day opposite the hotel where a large crowd had assembled to see who would carry off the $75 breech-loader. They had broken seven yeast powder bottles each and Dixson had followed it with his eighth, when his brother shot and apparently missed. The bottle was picked up and behold! All the shot was in the bottle. It had entered at the mouth and not broken it. Dixson was awarded the gun.

The Post Office has been moved. "Don't it look funny in Shinn's store now?" is the common remark.

S. Seug

CHURCH DEDICATION

The New M.E. Church at Port Norris Formally Given to God's Service - The Whole Debt Provided for.

Liberal Givers

About the best thing we could have heard in the line of Church work, was that accomplished at Port Norris, on Sunday last, when the entire indebtedness of the church property, mortgage on the land, debt on the new building and all, was raised and the handsome structure handed over to the trustees with not one dollar of encumbrance resting against it. Of all the church organizations far or near, that we have knowledge of; the old Methodist Episcopal Church Society at Port Norris was the most unfortunate. Resting on the verge of bankruptcy for a long time, in the hands of the Sheriff, we believe, more than once, and finally burned to the ground its lot was indeed a hard one and fairly excited the sympathy of all. On the day of the dedication of the present edifice – last Sunday - $2,150.00 was raised throughout the day, which amount cancelled the debt resting against the church, but there was still $150.00 mortgage on the ground to be provided for, which was left for the evening meeting. At that service Doctor Thomas Hanlon and Reverend Mr. Corbet, of New York again presented the case to the liberal givers, and $500.00 more was raised or $350.00 more than required to pay the whole indebtedness. Our informant says: "They just give and give almost without asking, and if they hadn't been stopped would perhaps have been giving yet." The citizens of Port Norris in general, and the members and organization of the Methodist Episcopal Church in particular are doubtless greatly grateful at the result, and they have our congratulations.

Church Dedicated at Port Norris

The handsome new Methodist Episcopal Church edifice at Port Norris was dedicated to the service of God on Sunday last, a large assemblage of people being present. Reverend Doctor Thomas Hanlon, one of the most eloquent ministers of the New Jersey Conference, now Principal of the Pennington Seminary, delivered an able sermon, as did also Reverend Mr. Corbett, of New York. Splendid music was rendered during the service by the choir. In the morning the statement was made to the effect that there was a debt of $2,300 against the lot and building. A collection was taken, when it was found that $2,150 had been secured. At the evening service $500 more were subscribed, thus cancelling the entire church indebtedness, and leaving a balance of $350. The proverbial generosity of the oystermen was well illustrated when the collections were taken, and they gave freely and cheerfully.

January 8

The Port Norris Bridge

The recent order of the Board of Freeholders to re-build the bridge at Mauricetown has settled the question as to its permanency, and it is well that such is the case. But, a bridge ought also to be built across the Maurice River at Port Norris, and if the members of the present Board of Freeholders will not appropriate the funds for its erection, then a straight issue should be made of the question at the spring elections. The bridge is needed, and sooner or later, it must come. It will be built this year, if the voters of Fairfield and Lawrence Townships do their duty in the election of Freeholders. A majority of the people of those Townships are favorable to the bridge, and they should see to it that Freeholders are chosen next March who will carry out their wishes. The time has gone by for dilatory movements in this matter, and the hour has arrived for energetic, active work on the part of every friend of the Port Norris Bridge.

January 9

A few evenings since at quite a late hour the melodious strains of the Port Norris Cornet Band were heard in front of the residence of the newly married couple, Mr. and Mrs. William B. Hand. After playing several pieces the band were invited in, where fine refreshments were served, and the boys departed, wishing the young couple many happy years. The band then proceeded to the residence of Mr. and Mrs. Samuel Loper, Jr., and it being very late, after giving these young people a fine little music, they returned to their homes.

Mr. Howard Sockwell is furnishing his new home with fine furniture.

The services of the week of prayer were held in both churches of our town.

The following Chiefs of Idaho tribe No. 51, Improved Order of Red Men, were installed into office last Friday evening by District Deputy Theodore Woodruff; Sachem, Joseph S. Turner; Senior Sagemore, A. Chester; Junior Sagemore, Charles Green; Chief of Records, L. M. Lee; Keeper of Wampum, Lucius E. Yates; Representative, Rueben W. Chamberlain.

Many visitors were in our town over the Sabbath attending the dedication of the Methodist Episcopal Church.

JO

January 13

High Winds

Oyster Boats Dragged On the Marshes at Long Reach

The high winds of Friday and Saturday did considerable damage to the vessel property alone. On Friday night the rain and hail came down in torrents. Boats that were anchored in the Maurice River were driven ashore and left high and dry upon the marsh. The storm, as described by one who weathered it all, was nearly as bad as the September gale a year or so back. Crews were on watch all night and only those vessels that had two anchors were at all safe while others were shooting and tossing about, and were at the mercy of the waves being run into with other vessels. Several boats are badly broken up by being run into with other vessels. Three or four are so far on the marshes that it will take some time to get them off. On Saturday night an owner of a boat came down from Philadelphia and drove to Back Creek to look after his oyster boat which had blown up on the marsh near Sea Breeze. What other damage has been done we are not appraised of. Nothing of any importance in this city, except the snow beating under roofs and damaging ceilings and goods, and limbs from trees blown off.

January 14

TROUT – In Port Norris, January 14, '86, Sarah T., wife of Job T. Trout, aged 47 years, 9 months.

The oyster industry is very slack. Some say the oysters are packed very badly "off shore," where they have never been known to pack before.

January 20

A horse belonging to John Hand, Jr., fell in a fit and died one day last week, while carting oysters.

Steve Mayhew took a wagon load of young ladies to Dividing Creek Saturday, skating. About one hundred and fifty were on the pond, including several from Newport and Haleyville and some of the best skaters of Port Norris, among them Reverend Lorenzo G. Appleby, T. Ferguson, James Greenley, C.W. Godfrey and others.

Mr. Charles P. Bacon has a cow which furnished him with two calves Monday night.

Herbert Harris moves to Bridgeton this week. He is in the employ of Superintendent Dowdney.

A sloop from New Haven, Connecticut, bound for North Carolina, is at the mouth of the river frozen in. A crew of six sporting men are in charge of her. They were caught in the gale of last Saturday night, and on account of the carrying away of their jib were unable to make the river until Saturday morning. They lost both anchors and the jib was torn into shreds.

The fishermen do not catch many now, although they fish day and night.

Only two boats were seen working in the cove Monday. Not many oysters are being shipped on account of the freeze up.

SKATER

January 21

The Maurice River was frozen solid the greater portion of the past week. Skating parties went from Mauricetown to Dorchester, Leesburg, Bricksboro, and other points on the river without much difficulty, and had lots of fun along the way. The ice was thick enough to bear loaded wagons and horses, which has not been the case before for several years.

January 28

Mrs. Mary Tribbett fell on the sidewalk recently and severely injured herself.

Miss Martha Tribbett has been confined to the house for three weeks with a sore throat. She is improving slowly.

Mrs. Silvia Jerrell had a stroke of palsy Friday afternoon and has since been unconscious.

One of our shippers lately received a postal which read as follows: "The last shipment received from you were frozen. They are too small for lime; Italians drink stale beer and what shall we do with them." He sent word back." "Make blue ink out of them."

Our population is rapidly increasing. Beside "transients" we have several very small residents of attractive demeanor. TEN

January 30

ONENS – In Port Norris, January 30, '86, Annie M., wife of John Onens, in the 25th year of her age.

February 1

Mrs. Elizabeth Chamberlain was buried Friday at Haleyville. The funeral sermon was preached at the new Methodist Episcopal Church here, this being the first funeral service in this building. She was about eighty years old.

Extra meetings are going on here in both churches, and we hear that the Salvation Army is coming soon.

A new school house in the spring is talked of.

Mr. William Bloxson, of Delaware, has just moved in on South Church Street, in one of Mr. John English's new houses.

Sore throats are quite plentiful here now.

February 3

Mrs. Annie Onens, the estimable young wife of John Onens, was buried at Port Norris on Tuesday. It was one of the largest funerals in Port Norris for a long time. The body was beautifully laid out, while many fragrant flowers, the tributes of loving hearts, surrounded the casket. Mrs. Onens was the daughter of Charles and Fanny Lake and had had a long illness.

February 6

McDANIELS – DILKS –At Dividing Creek, February 6th, by the Reverend W. Cattell, Mr. Willard S. McDaniels, of Port Norris, and Miss Amy Dilks of Dividing Creek.

February 13

The Floods at Port Norris

The floods in and near Port Norris did damage estimated at not less than $400. Just below the residence of Mr. George Robbins it was found necessary to erect a temporary bridge, twenty feet long, over the road. The roadway at Peter's Run was washed out and in a number of other places was put in bad condition. It is said that there are not a dozen cellars in Port Norris which do not contain more or less water, some of them full and running out on the Street. The female portion of the inhabitants who own gum boots make daily and graceful pilgrimages to the cellar in them. Frank Howard's wood pile started off on a sailing expedition of its own and though lost to sight is to memory dear.

At Long Reach, strange to say, no damage was done, though if the tide had been higher there would undoubtedly have been considerable of it. The washout at Kinney's Branch on the Cumberland and Maurice River Railroad has been repaired and trains are now running on time.

February 18

The recent freshet did considerable damage at Port Norris. A large number of cellars were filled with water, while wood piles, lumber, etc., were set afloat in various parts of the town. The road near George Robbins' residence was badly flooded, and it became necessary to erect a bridge twenty feet long for the accommodation of pedestrians. At Kinney's Branch on the Cumberland and Maurice River railroad, near Haleyville, a portion of the road bed and track was washed away.

February 22

A large number of persons were baptized at the Baptist Church yesterday, some in the morning and some in the evening.

Extra meetings are still in progress at the Methodist Episcopal Church. Several have joined on probation and quite a number are still seeking.

The carpenters have commenced to build the new store for Firman Campbell, of Port Elizabeth. It is to be on Main Street near the run.

Mr. W. Willard McDaniels, of Port Norris, and Miss Amy Dilks, of Dividing Creek were married recently at the latter place.

E. J. Cook has bought the old Sharp place, opposite the Baptist Church, of Thomas Hand for $1100.

The wish is expressed by many that a letter box could be placed on the corner of Main and Bacon Streets for the accommodation of persons in that end of the town. The Post Office is a long distance off now. The mail agent lives on Bacon Street, and could carry the mail from the box, as he would goes by each day, without any trouble. It would be a great accommodation to the place. Another place where it is suggested where a box might advantageously be put up is in the neighborhood of where the old Post Office was located.

February 23

The Baptist Church was filled to overflowing, both morning and evening, to witness the ordinance of Baptism. The pulpit was occupied at both services by the Reverend M. M. Finch of Pennsylvania, former pastor of this church. He made some excellent points on the subject of Moral Character. After the morning service eight candidates were baptized by Reverend Finch. After the evening service twelve, by Reverend Mr. Lorenzo Appleby, the present pastor.

Misses Ella and Anna Booblitz and Miss Lizzie Pyle, of Bridgeton, made a flying visit to Mrs. William Hand, sister of the latter lady.

Some ladies from your city and Port Norris took a trip to Long Reach the other day and by the kindness of Mr. John Broadwater were invited to a treat of oysters in the cabin of an oyster boat. You must not ask us how many they eat!

Miss Nellie Ware, who has been in Washington, D.C., the greater part of a year, is still there. Her many friends are getting very anxious to see her pleasant face again and are wondering when she will return. She must certainly be having a good time.

JUMBO

March 3

The annual meeting of the Maurice River Cove and Delaware Bay Oyster Association will be held at Port Norris, on Monday, March 15th, at 10 o'clock, A.M. Business of importance will be transacted.

March 4

March came in with us with such a blast that our oystermen have been compelled to remain at home.

Twenty-six persons received the right hand of fellowship at the Baptist Church last Sabbath morning and two candidates were baptized in the evening. The extra meetings at this church have closed for present. Much good was done through them.

Mr. George Lucas, of Newport has just moved in part of Mr. Collins house on Walnut Street.

Mr. Hugh Hand and wife have returned home to Camden, after a visit to friends and relatives in this city.

Mr. Theodore Moncrief, of Newport, is visiting his brother and others of this place.

Monday evening fifty-five persons, mostly members of the Baptist Church, dropped in on Mr. Ellis Hand. They brought him and his wife many useful articles and a purse of money amounting to $22 and had refreshments and a jolly good time. Mr. Hand is an excellent man and has proven an extremely good sexton. The presents were given as a token of appreciation of his services during the extra meetings.

JUMBO

March 6

Launching at Port Norris 11:00 AM

The "Elvina E. Schoch," a handsome schooner built by William E. Parsons for Captain Leonard Hand, was launched at 9:45 this morning. She has a 46 foot keel and is intended for the oyster trade.

The Oyster Association

The Delaware Bay and Maurice River Cover Oyster Association held its annual meeting at Port Norris Monday. Captain L. D. Paynter was chosen chairman and Captain Benjamin F. Ogden secretary. James Fox was chosen special officer and Benjamin Campbell collector. The following auditing committee was chosen: William H. Berry, Edward D. Fleetwood, Benjamin F. Ogden, John W. Harris and Thomas A. Cruse. The auditing committee met and organized by the election of Captain William H. Berry as chairman and Captain Edward D. Fleetwood secretary. It was ordered that the annual statement be published in the *Dollar Weekly News* and *Bridgeton Pioneer*.

March 24

The temperance oystermen claim a victory in electing special officer James Fox, of Cedarville, at Port Norris last week.

The high winds are causing a great scarcity of oysters.

March 25

WHAT THEY SAY

Edwin M. Ware, Port Norris:

"This has been a very hard winter on oysters. I don't suppose so many have died for many years as during the past winter. During the last month or more, good ones have been very scarce. Planting begins first of April and then we have to get them as best we can."

A leading Bridgeton Merchant:

"I am satisfied that the daily and weekly *NEWS* are unquestionably the best advertising mediums in town. We may think your prices a little "steep" sometimes but still we find it pays better in the end."

Reverend J. R. Thompson, Port Norris' new Methodist Episcopal minister, preached very acceptably to his charge on Sunday last.

The Maurice River Cove and Delaware Bay Oyster Association is in excellent financial condition. According to the report of the Auditing Committee, the Association had received during the year $3,416.03 for licenses from 394 oyster sloops and schooners. On March 15, 1886, there was a balance of $1,092.90 in collector Benjamin F. Campbell's hands. This is a good showing, and is satisfactory evidence that the affairs of the Association have been well and economically managed.

April 1

Reverend J. R. Thompson, the new pastor of the Methodist Episcopal Church, at Port Norris, will preach a course of sermons to young men, beginning with Sunday next, April 4th. Subject: "What the age demands." A cordial invitation is extended to the young men of the village to be present.

April 2

Two more new stores in the place. Mr. Firman Campbell has his new store finished and opened. Mr. David Lake has been away purchasing goods for his new store this week.

Mrs. David T. Robbins started yesterday for her spring millinery goods.

The oystermen are busy as bees now and not at all sorry to see the pleasant weather.

All Fool's Day passed off rather quietly here, although a number of amusing practical jokes were played.

A new hall is talked of by our lodges. We hope talk won't be all.

April 7

Some large vessels are now lying at Long Reach with oysters brought from Virginia flats.

April 9

Port Norris is well represented at Salvation meetings held in Dividing Creek.

Mrs. Ogden Burt is quite sick. Doctor Henry C. Fithian attending.

Mr. James Stout moved to Bridgeton last week.

Mr. George Robbins, Jr., has another fine son.

April 10

The oyster sloop "William Dennis" was launched at Long Reach at 10 o'clock this morning. She was built by William E. Parsons and is owned by Messr. Lucius, John and William Yates, of Port Norris, and William Dennis, of Philadelphia.

April 15

Mr. George Sloan, Sr., of Dividing Creek, has leased the house and property of Richard Robbins, of Bridgeton, for five years. He is having a new portico added to the building.

Mr. Brunyate is having his house re-painted in a clear color.

Mr. Timothy Bateman has a new house commenced on High street.

Mr. Aquilla Miller has the cellar dug for his new house on the corner of Brown and Bacon streets.

April 24

Miss Carrie Bateman, daughter of Timothy Bateman, of Port Norris, is paying Bridgeton a visit to-day. She graduates from the State Normal school, at Trenton on June next, and is at home on a two weeks' vacation.

April 28

Several new houses are going up in Port Norris. Our thriving village promises at no distant day to be one of the liveliest towns in South Jersey.

Easter Sunday was a success at the Methodist Episcopal Church.

Miss Lizzie Bacon is preparing for a concert which, it is thought, will be a grand success.

Howard Kemble has bought the *Dollar Weekly News* route in Port Norris and solicits items of news as well as subscribers.

April 29

Mr. Samuel R. Mayhew has purchased the hack line of D. B. Ferguson and is having it newly fitted up for the accommodation of the public.

Doctor Henry C. Fithian has been beautifying the lawn in front of his residence.

Mr. Dansee, the photographer, will leave for Pennsgrove in a few days. He speaks of the village being a money making place.

We are glad to see the smiling countenance of Miss Mellie Chambers once more, after her brief visit to her father at Newport

April 30

Mr. H. H. Nickelson paid Bridgeton a flying visit yesterday. Miss Lizzie Bacon is visiting Philadelphia for a few days. Mr. E. M. Fithian visited Port Norris yesterday. Mr. John Dunham, butcher, of Alloway, was in town yesterday. Mr. John English, of Philadelphia, is visiting, William Brunyate.

Mr. R. D. James and son, from Dennisville, are building a very pretty house just above the Methodist Episcopal Church which, when finished, will be their home.

The Salvation Army was to hold an open air meeting last Saturday evening, but owing to rain was compelled to seek shelter. Doctor Stetson Bacon very cheerfully donated his veranda for them to hold their meeting under and they accidentally broke one of the large windows in his drug store.

Mr. Stanford has placed in front of his place of business, on Main Street, a very pretty lamp.

Mr. D. B. Ferguson was on a fishing expedition yesterday and captured two dozen nice rock fish.

Miss Hattie Bloxsom, daughter of our townsman Robert Bloxsom, and who is being educated at the Nebinger College, at Philadelphia, spent her Easter vacation at home.

Mr. Howard Ware, of the firm of Ware & Trask, visited Port Norris yesterday.

Mr. Thomas P. Covington, of the firm of Covington & Patterson, of Philadelphia, is spending a few days in the "Oyster City."

May 1

The carpenters and masons are both busy just now in rebuilding and repairing houses. Joseph Onens has the contract to build a commodious dwelling house for Timothy Bateman. Dixon & Sheldon have contracted to do the mason work.

Mr. William Brunyate is having his home repainted. Mr. Woodruff, from Bridgeton, is doing the work. He certainly knows how to make an old house look good as new.

Mrs. Edwin M. Ware is reported a little better although still very sick.

May 5

The Cedarville and Port Norris Baptist Sunday schools have exchanged libraries, and now the scholars of each school rejoice in the possession of new books.

May 6

The annual meeting for the election of officers of the Cumberland and Maurice River Railroad Company was held at the Hotel de Middleton on Monday A.M. The party, many of whom were from Philadelphia, came down on a special train. The annual report of business of the year compared favorably with past years. The company was sumptuously provided for at Middleton House. After a speech or two by members of the board, the party returned at 3:20 expressing themselves well pleased with Port Norris, where doubtless, their future meetings will be held.

As we have seen no mosquito items we hasten to make one. They have come and seem to refer to others that are coming. They sing in a high key and seem healthy.

May 8

Warrington L. Hand has embarked in the ice cream and fruit business. His new saloon presents an attractive appearance.

There has been an immense quantity of oysters planted thus far the present season. We learn that at least ten thousand dollars have been expended in this business by one company and still the work goes on. Should they meet no misfortune it looks as if we should be prepared to satisfy all reasonable demands for oysters during next season at least.

The old board of Officers of the Cumberland and Maurice River Railroad were re-elected at the annual meeting held at Port Norris on Monday.

May 11

Joseph Onens has about got the frame for Timothy Bateman's house pointing skyward. This house is 19 feet posts and is on a high wall. When completed it will be a credit to Port Norris.

Edward Conahay has by the addition to his house helped the looks of his place, as well as made more room.

Mr. Daniel Blackman, and his sister, Miss Annie, spent Sunday at their father's in this place.

There is some talk of a new Post Office building here. The office is now in front room of Mr. Lambert's house.

F.D.

May 13

Port Norris will have a gala time on the Fourth of July. The congregation of the Methodist Episcopal Church have taken the matter in hand, and propose to show the county that the patriotic spirit of our Revolutionary fathers is not yet dead in Port Norris and vicinity. The Committee of Arrangements will secure a first class speaker for the occasion, and one of the best bands of music that can be found.

May 15

Captains Charles Peace and William Fowler have improved their property by new fences.

Miss Roxie Corson, who has been teaching school here since September last, leaves this afternoon for her home in Petersburg, Cape May County. Her many friends in Port Norris are very sorry, school closes very early, but hope to see Miss Corson in September again.

A few friends of Mrs. Charles Peace, of Port Norris, surprised her on the anniversary of her birthday, May 12th. She received several very handsome presents which gratified her very much. All spent a very enjoyable evening and after refreshments were served they separated, feeling very much pleased with the pleasures of the occasion.

NEWS BOY

May 19

Corson Socwell, of Port Norris, has accepted a position as steward of the "John A. Warner." This makes his fourth season on the "Warner."

The new oyster laws governing the Maurice River Cove and Delaware Bay are the best the oysterman have ever had. By their enforcement numbers of foreign vessels have been driven out of the cove and bay, so that the business is entirely in the hands of residents of this State. This is as it should be. Now, the Oyster Association should built a steamer as a guard boat for the coast, have her well manned and armed, and thus stop the stealing of oysters committed by certain parties whom the present guard boat (a sailing vessel) cannot reach.

May 20

PETERSON-BOWEN – At Port Norris on the 27th of March, 1886 by Reverend J. R. Thompson, William Peterson, to Miss Emma Bowen, both of Port Norris.

A revised edition of the Oyster Laws governing Maurice River Cove and Delaware Bay has been printed in book form, and can now be had by oystermen who may apply to Benjamin Campbell, collector of the oyster fund, at Long Reach, Port Norris.

GREENLEE – TROUT – At Port Norris, May 23rd by Reverend Lorenzo G. Appleby, James S. Greenlee and Miss Lizzie Trout.

May 25

Another wedding in our place, Mr. James S. Greenlee and Miss Lizzie Trout were married on Saturday. Reverend Mr. Lorenzo Appleby, of the Baptist church, performed the ceremony.

Mr. Henry Ager has another fine son. Mr. West Hiles must also be added to the list of happy men.

Port Norris, we believe, has a representative or two on the excursion to Gettysburg.

Matters quiet down here. The strawberry succeeds the oyster in popular favor.

I.C.U.

May 28

Mr. George W. Sloan's new house is finished and he and his family moved in it yesterday, from Dividing Creek.

The death of Mrs. Edwin M. Ware has caused much sadness here. The interment will take place in Bridgeton.

The new Post Office is nearly enclosed.

Mr. Howard Socwell was brought home today. He had got caught in a main sail and was considerably bruised.

R.

May 31

Mr. Lorenzo Parks' funeral took place Saturday.

Mr. William Loller has accepted a position as inspector of fruit jars lids at Sharon Hill, Pennsylvania.

The Methodist Episcopal Church is being handsomely painted and other improvements are also to be made to it.

Friday and Saturday evenings the American Mechanics' festival in the town hall was largely attended and a large sum was realized in the way of profits, by the Order.

A marriage will take place on Tuesday, June 1st, between Mr. M. Usinger and Miss Hannah English, both of Clayton.

A set-to took place between Duff Long and Pat Moore, the sugar mill wonders. Long got knocked out in one round.

June 3

Mr. Stephen R. Mayhew's elegant new hack was put on yesterday and was christened by taking a party of his friends around the town. Mr. Mayhew is ready now to accommodate the travelling public and will meet all trains.

Mr. Seth Tribbett is building a temporary "Opera House" for Miss Lizzie Bacon. The "opera" is to consist of tableaux and dramas to be played by her pupils.

Miss Nellie Chambloss has resigned her position as postmistress. The vacancy is to be filled by Miss Fox.

We are very sorry to learn that Mr. Joseph Stanford, one of our most enterprising business men, is on the sick list.

Mr. Pink Tudas, our accommodating hack driver, has returned after a week's vacation among the Bridgeton ladies.

Mr. John C. Hand has built a very neat fence in front of his residence on Main Street.

William S. Lambert, Postmaster, is building a new post office next door to George Owen's dry goods house.

The Methodists are making extensive preparations for Children's Day.

WARE – At Port Norris, on Wednesday, May 26th, 1886, Rebecca W., wife of Edwin M. Ware.

O.K.

June 5

The funeral of the late Mrs. Edwin M. Ware, of Port Norris, took place this morning from the residence of Mr. A. S. Emmell, on West Commerce Street, Bridgeton. It was largely attended. A number came from Washington and other points on the morning train. Reverends Coyle and Belden officiated in the services at the house and Reverends Coyle and Huff at the grave. The body was interred in the Broad Street cemetery.

June 10

The Fourth at Port Norris

The Knights of the Mystic Chain will celebrate the Fourth of July at Port Norris. They intend to out do any celebration ever held in that place. One of the features of the occasion will be the initiation of a candidate or "the secrets of the order exposed." Further notice will be given in this paper, and everybody should be on the lookout for it.

Mrs. Elizabeth McConnell, who has been spending about a month in Bridgeton, with Mrs. Richard Robbins on South Laurel Street, returned home to this place this morning.

June 11

The Port Norris folks will witness a big time in Robbins' grove on the 12th instant; The National Cornet Band of that place will hold a grand picnic. There will be much fun.

June 12

Annual Picnic at Port Norris

All Port Norris was aglow on Saturday last, the occasion being the grand annual picnic which the people of that village hold every year about this time. It was held in the grove near the school house all day, the gayest time being in the evening. Music was furnished by the Ariel Cornet Band of that place and an orchestra composed of Messrs. Shores, Carll and Johnson of Bridgeton and Messrs. Landwhir, of Camden, and Stefano, of Philadelphia. The different tables "groaned" under their weight of cake, candies, nuts, etc. In the evening the grove was lighted and was literally thronged with men, women and children.

The orchestra kept a continual playing and was applauded by all. The speaker of the occasion was Reverend Mr. J. R. Thompson of Port Norris, who addressed the picnickers in his usual good style. He commenced by complimenting the musicians and referred to, the greatest musician of the age, Mendelsasohn, and others; said that music of any kind from a Jew's harp to a piano had the greatest charms for him, except one which he never could appreciate: "that one was when my dear old mother used to lay me across her knee and the sounds which vibrated then had no charms for me." He advocated music in the churches and thought that in no place under God's command should there be more of it than in the church. The speaker was humorous in his remarks and greatly pleased the audience with the speech. After he had finished, the Ariel band played two or three times while the auctioneer was busy in disposing of the few things which were left on the table and then the picnic of 1886 was closed, every one having had a good time and a good word for everybody.

June 14

Children's Day at Port Norris

Seldom, if ever, was a church more beautifully decorated than was the Methodist Episcopal. The floral designs consisted of two "Gates Ajar," one at the right of the pulpit, of water lilies, the other at the left, of carnations and evergreens and between the two, in the centre of the pulpit was a cross of solid magnolias; in the background over the pulpit were the words in letters made of evergreen "Children's Day." At the service in the morning the pastor of the church preached from the 2d chapter of Exodus and the 6th verse. The rite of Baptist was administered in the morning. The evening was the time set apart for the children's exercise, which was opened by an organ voluntary by Master George Thompson; singing by the choir and prayer by Reverend Lorenzo G. Appleby. Mr. Joseph Lee then made an address. He showed he had spared no pains to make it a success. The program consisted of singings and recitations. All well rendered and very enjoyable.

A most excellent closing address was made by Miss Mattie Lee. Reverend J. H. Thompson deserves great credit for the pains he has taken in training both choir and school.

J.C. Sutton and Belford, two enterprising young men have purchased the butcher shop of Sheppard Robbins, formerly owned by C.B. Shaw, and are doing business here.

The Cumberland County Society meets in the Methodist Episcopal Church Thursday afternoon at 3 o'clock.

June 15

Doctor Henry C. Fithian has now completed fixing up his drug store. The Doctor and his good wife have excellent taste.

Mrs. Frank Howard, wife of conductor Howard, and children are visiting Philadelphia.

Asher Robbins spent Sunday with us for the first time since he returned from the west.

The attractions are so great up the street around the corner for a young Bridgeton gentleman that on Saturday about 6 pm, he strolled off and was not heard from until 4 pm Sunday. The proprietor and inmates of his boarding house were much alarmed for fear something serious has happened. They were about to hunt for him when to their great joy they received an order from him for his trunk to be sent as he was going to change his boarding house. The proprietor being absent at the time the inmates of the house very kindly engaged Mr. Tudas to deliver said trunk. At the latest accounts he was in his new boarding house, happy as a clam at high tide.

June 16

John R. Lake's horse, while at work in the field, to a harror, at Port Norris the other day, indulged in a little pleasure excursion on its own account. Dr. Henry C. Fithian sewed up the wounds.

June 21

Children's Day was celebrated at the Port Norris Baptist Church last evening. The church was beautifully decorated with flowers, birds, etc. This was the finest display ever seen in Port Norris. There were three arches crossing the church, decorated with flowers on a background of white cloth and containing the words "Welcome Visitors," and "Children's Day." Back in the pulpit was arranged a throne set in an arch trimmed in flowers and greens. On the top of it was placed "The Word of God" and under this was a large open bible. The Methodists, by invitation, joining in the celebration the house was literally packed. The exercises opened by singing "Hear our Prayers," choir: followed by scripture reading, Mr. W. Henry Berry; prayer, Reverend J. R. Thompson; singing, school: recitation, "Children's Day," Charlie Robbins; recitation. "The Greeting," Emma B. Robbins; singing "Our Little Ones, Amy Kimble; recitation "What will you give?" three boys and three girls; recitation, Edith Cook; singing by choir with alto solo; Object Flower Lesson, eight girls; singing, Mrs. Bateman's class, recitation, Bertha Hanes; recitation, Sophie Robbins; singing, "Redemption's Story," school; blackboard exercise, a lesson on flowers, Mary Kemble; recitation, Walter Pashley; duet, Mary and Lizzie Lambert; recitation, "The Sunday School" Lizzie Garrison; recitation, "Honoring Parents," Nellie Whitaker; singing, choir; blackboard exercise, Master Richard Lore; recitation, little Anna Kimble; duet, Mary and Lizzie Lambert; recitation, Ruth Robbins ; singing choir; recitation, little Mary Terry; singing; choir; recitation, Eva Fisher; recitation; Laura Hignutt; the annual letter, Phebe Gaskill; address, Reverend J.R. Thompson; bass solo, "The Raining Deep," Mr. Hankins, of South Jersey Institute, crowning of the angel of the Sunday school," four young ladies and one young man, collection; "Blest be the Tie that binds," school; benediction.

June 30

William F. Jones, who graduated from Pennington, last week, is in Bridgeton visiting his friends, prior to taking his new charge in Missouri. Stephen Campbell, of Port Norris, who graduated at the same time, also has a charge in Missouri and goes with him. Mr. Campbell was at one time in the employ of C. W. Shoemaker, in Bridgeton.

The tug "Schuyler" will make an excursion from Port Norris to Millville, next Monday, arriving in time to take in the parade, bicycle race, &c.

July 1

Big Time at Port Norris

The Knights of the Mystic Chain intend to make Port Norris ring with patriotic enthusiasm on Saturday, July 3rd, in honor of the 110th anniversary of American Independence. They propose to have a grand street parade in the morning, followed by an address on the day and the society by John W. Newlin, Esquire, editor of the *Millville Republican.* In the afternoon, the renowned orator, "Honorable Cupo Caesar Clemuel Bunng," will discourse to the multitude on the glorious Fourth, and the reasons why it is celebrated. Dinner will be served in the grove, and all the delicacies of the season furnished. The National Cornet Band will furnish the music throughout the day. There will be sports of various kinds and character, and balloon ascension. All who wish a good time on the Fourth will do well to spend it in the land of the Maurice River Cove Oyster, for the Knights of the Mystic Chain propose doing things up brown. The trains of the Cumberland and Maurice River Railroad will take you to Port Norris on that day on prompt time and special rates.

Mr. Edward M. Ware, of Port Norris was in Bridgeton this morning.

July 4

The Fourth at Port Norris

Port Norris, in common with the other towns hereabouts, celebrated the Fourth on Monday, and it had a big time. The celebration was under the auspices of Castle Number 7 of the Knights of the Mystic Chain and in a very creditable manner indeed was it carried out.

The early salute was fired from twelve pound cannon. John W. Newlin, of Millville, was the orator in the morning and made an excellent address. Music was furnished by the National Cornet Band, of Port Norris, and there was good vocal music by the choir. The parade was a large and fine one. The different orders and citizens and Sunday schools generally turned out. The Declaration of Independence was read by William Hand.

In the afternoon Reverend Mr. J.R. Thompson, of Port Norris, made an able speech and persons enjoyed themselves in various ways, and in the evening there was a mock imitation which as one expressed it, was "as good as a circus." The "Honorable "Cupo Caesar Clemuel Bungg," of Topeker, got off a comical speech and the sending upward of two balloons closed the festivities. Altogether it was a very enjoyable day and one that will not be soon forgotten.

The celebration at Port Norris was a "boss" affair, a large number of people taking part in the exercises of the day. The brass gun from the State Arsenal made the welkin ring all day with its booming thunder.

July 16

Mr. Charles Harris' new house was raised on Wednesday, on Chestnut Street. Mr. Henry Robbins has one nearly enclosed opposite Mr. Harris.'

Mr. Hammett Lake was presented with a fine son last Saturday.

Timothy Bateman's and Edward Stites' new houses are nearly done and they are both very nice ones.

X.Y.

July 21

We regret to learn of the illness of Mrs. Benjamin Campbell, of Port Norris. She has been out of her head since Sunday, caused; it is believed, by worry over the burning of her store some two months ago. At last accounts she was resting more easily, though still showing signs of mental trouble.

July 22

The *Port Norris Gazette* is the name of a new paper which has just made its appearance in the thriving oyster town at the terminus of the Cumberland and Maurice River Railroad. The proprietors are William B. Hand and Lorenzo G. Appleby.

Captain Edward Stites, of the firm of Stites and Son, oyster shippers, at Long Reach, Port Norris, has recently erected for himself a very handsome residence. The parlors are finished in solid walnut and ash, with plate glass window centres, ornamented with colored trimmings. The house is one of the finest and best in Port Norris.

July 25

The *Port Norris Gazette* is the latest candidate for public favor.
William B. Hand and Reverend Lorenzo G. Appleby are the editors
and publishers. We wish it all manner of success.

William F. Jones, of Bridgeton, and Stephen B. Campbell, of Port
Norris, two graduates of Pennington, leave today for Missouri
where they will engage in missionary work.

A buggy containing man, women and child, of Port Norris, struck
the pile of dirt in front of where the "arcade" stood, on North Pearl
Street, Saturday evening and the three were thrown out.
Fortunately no one was hurt and, as we understand it, no blame is
attached to anyone.

July 26

Considerable interest was taken in the game of ball here on Saturday last between the Up-town and Down-town nines. It started out to be a very fair game but soon was like the handle of a jug – all on one side. Fisher had a hand injured by a hard-knocked ball and the Up-towners lost a valuable player. Mr. Edward Stites officiated as umpire and gave general satisfaction. Following is the score.

DOWN-TOWN NINE

	O.	R.
J. Compton, p.	1	4
R. Dubois, c	4	2
J. Lee, s.s.	3	3
S. Robbins, 1 b.	1	5
W. Yates, 2b.	1	4
B. Harris, 3 b.	2	4
Geo. Lee, l.f.	2	4
W. Fowler. c.f.	2	3
J. Gibson, r.f.	2	3
	18	32

UP-TOWN NINE

	O.	R.
L. Harris, p	2	0
J. Rowley, c	1	2
J. MaConald, s.s	3	0
G. McGee, 1 b	2	1
S. Green, 2 b.	2	1
G. Simpson, 3 b	2	0
C. Fisher, l.f.	2	0
H. Pierson, c.f.	1	1
E. Riggins, r.f.	<u>3</u>	<u>0</u>
	18	5

The down-town and up-town base ball nines at Port Norris played again on Friday and Saturday. Friday's score, 28 to 4, Saturday's 32 to 5, both in favor of the down-towners.

DOWN TO PORT NORRIS

A "NEWS" MAN'S TRIP ON THE SNORTING "MASHEEN" YESTERDAY

The Large Hearted Ex-Sheriff's Trials and Tribulations – Sanguinary Battles – Picturesque Port Norris, Many Improvements

Even a newspaper man can afford an occasional *free* excursion, and so yesterday we boarded Dowdney's big wagon for a trip to Port Norris. The ex sheriff is a good talker, and it is a real treat to be one of two (the Sheriff or the other fellow) to fill the rear seat of his comfortable caboose and hear him spin yearns while the "masheen" goes plunging madly along past farms, forests, towns and hamlets on its way to the Port.

A well-posted and thoroughly informed man is the ex-Sheriff, whose opportunities for getting a glimpse at the inside wrinkle that furor the corrugated brow of troubled humanity have been varied and many. Once elected sheriff from this county and twice a representative to the lower branch of N.J. House of Representatives and now Superintendent of the Cumberland and Maurice River Railroad, beside filling a host of minor "gifts" which he himself could not recall, it would be strange indeed if this public functionary should he tongue tied in the presence of others. But enough of this.

We left Bridgeton, *i.e.* the sheriff and we, with not over 40 passengers on board and were reinforced at every station along the way down. At Fairton, our first stopping place, we were boarded by not less than 300 passengers – a horrid old grumbler on the side aisle said 3,000,000 – every last one of which was a dead head. Everybody acquainted with the large hearted Superintendent of this road is aware that more persons are dead headed on the Cumberland and Maurice River Railroad than any other line heading out of Bridgeton, but this overflow was too much even for Dowdney, and he "kicked,' or more literally true perhaps "fit." In this he was joined by the other passengers and the invaders were glad to escape by whatever means possible, out of the windows or else-where some with broken lips, mashed heads, etc.

This fight with precisely similar results was re-enacted at every stopping place along the road going and returning.

The old "deckers" say this sanguinary fight has prevailed the season through, and that much gore has been shed.

Port Norris is one of those long-drawn out Jersey towns that you sometimes hear tell of, such as Berlin (formerly Long a Coming), Long Branch, Greenwich, Cedarville, and numberless others. It is pretty, though, every foot of this long street, and when one has travelled from above the Methodist Episcopal Church to its finale below Robbinstown the wish often expressed is that it was "twice as long." But, then, Port Norris isn't comprised in this one main street by any means, and it is really a vigorous, growing little town all over. The one long row of houses on the Main Street reminds one greatly of Pearl Street above Michel's store, and some of these houses are really handsome. Mr. Edward Stites, formerly living at Newport, is now finishing a house that will be really beautiful.

Externally the dwelling is of the most modern finish and will receive three coats of paint at the hands, or brush, of "near the bridge," T. Woodruff, of Bridgeton. The interior finish is to be of hard wood with ornate decorations overhead. The wall will be covered with the best gold embossed paper, and, in short, the dwelling will be a real "stunner" throughout.

This article should be sawed off right here, but we can't help saying that the improvements most noticed, not noted, are just below the unregenerated bridge to the left going down. Here are restaurants, confectionery stands, shoe shop, hardware store, etc., most of them standing, like some of the old houses in Venice, on piling above the water. We had a brief talk with friend, Samuel Foster, the man who when a candidate for office never solicited a vote for himself and who attended prayer meeting the night of election; a man who is ready and willing to be cursed for opposing the curse of intemperance, and who we hope through Providence to send to the state capital to represent us next winter.

July 29

Quite a number went to the "City by the Sea" on the Veterans' excursion yesterday. They all say the day was simply "immense."

Mr. Gus Henry and wife have gone over in Delaware to spend a few weeks.

Miss Anna Shaw, from County Seat, is stopping for a few days with Adam Vale, of the "Oyster City."

Hot is no name for it down here. Even the many breezes with which we are blessed have not sufficed to keep one in a comfortable state this week.

July 30

Two nines at Port Norris, styling themselves the up-town and down-town nines, played a game of ball on Wednesday afternoon, resulting in a victory for the down-towns by a score of 3 to 0. Dubois and Robbins were the victors' battery.

July 31

A new fence beautifies the property of Theophilus Newcomb and George Sloan.

Mr. Aquilla Miller moves into his handsome new home on Friday next.

Mr. Eli T. Robbins and family, of Bridgeton, are enjoying the fresh berries of Port Norris.

Matters unusually quiet down here.

Mrs. Franklin E. Hand, of Camden, is spending a few days with her sister's friends here.

Mr. Amos Pepper, of Dividing Creek, has bought two nice building lots on Washington Street above Brown, on which he intends building as soon as possible and moving down here. We are confident he will build a nice dwelling.

Mrs. Charles Harris and Miss Kate Campbell boarded the train yesterday afternoon, for a visit at Newport.

August 2

Mrs. Gille Lake died last Sunday morning, and is to be buried at the Methodist Episcopal Cemetery. Meet at the house at 10 o'clock Tuesday morning.

Mr. Howard Sockwell and wife and Robert L. Lake and wife have just returned from Philadelphia, Trenton, &c.

Mr. Edward Stites moved in his new house on Saturday.

Misses Bloxsom, Ross, Hutcheson, Harper, Mathews and Kemble, of Port Norris, all paid a flying visit to Miss Nellie Chambers, of Newport, on Saturday afternoon, in Mr. Stephen R. Mayhew's new hack. All enjoying it very much.

August 4

Captain Andrew Vail is going to start out on a pleasuring party today, to stay about 4 days. Captain Lemuel Robbins and William Snell, Major McDaniels, Charles Terry and some from Philadelphia are some of the party. They are going all around, to the boat races, fishing banks, Cape May and several other places.

The funeral of Mrs. Gille Lake was largely attended yesterday. Age 21 years.

Mr. David Hollinger has put a new portico to his house which is quite an improvement and an accommodation for his boarders.

Mr. Henry Robbins' new house, on Chestnut Street, is getting the painters' finishing touches. Mr. John Moncrief is to move in the last of this week.

August 5

Middletown Morsels

A stranger in town. He puts up on Green streets.

Henry Hasher and wife have moved in part of Joshua Nickerson's house.

Miss Susan Thompson, of Millville, is visiting at George Sayre's.

Chicken thieves are on the route now.

There was a general turnout on Sunday for the camp at Port Elizabeth. The schooner Polka started Monday on a pleasuring trip, en route to Philadelphia.

August 6

Quite a number went from here yesterday to Pierce's Point to witness the boat race.

Mr. Theophilus Newcomb is painting his new fence.

Quite a good many are carting dirt, filling up their door yards, side walks, &c.

The marsh is too wet to cart hay.

Mr. William Hollinger has been treating himself to a buggy. No doubt but the girls will go riding now soon.

Miss Emma Terry is visiting friends and relatives at Millville and Seaville.

August 7

FISHER-TRIBITT- At Port Norris, Saturday, Aug. 7, 1886, by
the Reverend J. R. Thompson, Elwood Fisher and Sarah Ann
Tribbett.

August 10

Last Saturday night, by Reverend Mr. J. R.Thompson, Mr. Elwood
Fisher and Miss Sarah Ann Tribbett were married, both of this
place.

On Thursday night Mr. Howard Dickson and Miss Sallie Perry
were married.

Reverend Mr. Lorenzo Appleby writes he will be back next
Sunday to preach for us again.

Each Sunday school has re-elected a committee to make
arrangements for their annual picnic.

There is a new fence around the Methodist Episcopal Cemetery.

Mr. George Webb and wife, and Gideon Webb and wife are on a
visit to Camden and other places. They went on a boat.

Mr. Leonard Hand tore away his old fence and put up a new and
fancy one and has built up his sidewalk.

Mr. Bacon has had his foundation laid and cellar dug for his new
house at the east end of the town.

Mr. Hugh H. Nickerson, our undertaker, has laid the foundation for
his work shop, &c. He is going to move it down over the bridge.

August 11

The Band boys went up to Middletown on Monday night and serenaded the newly married Mr. and Mrs. Elwood Fisher. They had a fine time.

Back street has had its name changed and is now "Christian."

Washington Street is being opened from Brown to Christian and a good many want Chestnut Street opened through from Bacon Street to Market Street. It ought to be.

Everything is quiet here.

Our enterprising butchers, Sutton & Harris say they have sold more meat last week since they have been in the business, they are going to enlarge their shop and fill in around it, and they have three horses and are going to get another.

Washington Street is being opened from Brown Street to Christian Street.

John Moncrief has move out of George Sloan's house into Henry Robbins' new house on Chestnut Street.

The "Samuel K. Dennis" is laying at the wharf with a load of packing hay. Some of the waterman have shown much interest in this craft, her captain says, because she was owned in Virginia and registered from Berlin, and it has been thought she would be taken to Virginia. She has now been changed, however, and hails from the port of Bridgeton.

The heavy rains have again filled our meadows and those that had corn planted will lose it by scalding.

The trustees of our public school are making preparations to have the school house fixed up for the fall term. Miss Lloyd of Glassboro is to take charge of the lower school.

Messrs. Banks and Shropshire have bought the sloop "Snow Flake" and are having her repaired and will put her in the salt trade with Captain A. Shropshire as master.

The colored camp meeting was well attended on Sunday. New Port, Cedarville, Port Norris, Mauricetown, Leesburg, Dorchester, Heislerville, Ewing's Neck and Millville being represented. It will be held over another week, meetings on Tuesday, Thursday and Saturday and Sunday nights.

The people here seem to be preparing for winter. The second vessel of coal has arrived this week for individual use.

John Heisler's old was horse Boney that served in the Rebellion died last Thursday. He had the U. S. on his shoulder and was about 30 years old we think he must be the last one of Uncle Sam's horses in Cumberland County as we know of no other, if there should be any left in Cumberland County we would like to hear from them through the *Chronicle.*

The National Cornet Band will go to Newport Thursday evening serenading. The band boys serenaded Elwood Fisher and wife, of Middletown, on Monday night. A large number of people from Port Norris were present and a good time is reported.

P.

August 12

The Haleyville and Port Norris base ball nines played a game last Saturday resulting in a victory for the Haleyville nine by a score of 9 to 0. Another game will be played next Saturday which is expected to be very interesting.

Separate passenger and freight trains now run on the Cumberland & Maurice River Railroad leaving here at 6:45 a.m. and 12:45 and 1:45 p.m.

August 13

Mr. Harrison Fleetwood and family arrived home Wednesday evening on the train. They have been away spending the summer.

Mr. Ludlum Lee is painting E. J. Cook's residence.

Miss Mattie Magee is very sick with typhoid fever.

The depot was half full of satchels, gunning and fishing apparatus Wednesday.

Bay parties are quite numerous here.

Captain Andrew Vail is going on a trip tomorrow and takes out a party.

The little base ball nine went to Dividing Creek Wednesday. They stood 5 to 5. Port Norris 2 innings and Creek 6; then the Creeks stopped and would not play as they saw they were getting beat.

Miss Emma Terry arrived home last evening.

August 14

We hear Reverend Mr. Lorenzo Appleby writes for a parsonage as he is to be married this fall. We have no doubt but that the church will build one just as soon as possible.

Mr. Elisha Reed lost his horse that he had in the parade on July 3. Mr. Henry Robbins' fine horse seems to be poisoned of foundered. His legs are breaking out in sores.

A stack of hay belonging to Mr. Joseph Onens was burned yesterday in a lot near his house. Some children set it on fire.

Blue fish bite first rate, but they are not a circumstance to the mosquitoes.

There is to be a boat race at Port Norris on the 26th instant, open to all sloops owned on the Maurice River. An entrance fee of $1 will be charged and entree should be made to Doctor Henry C. Fithian or Thomas Hand, with name of boat and owner, and entrance fee. All the money raised in entrance fees and subscriptions is to be given as prizes.

Daniel Bennett and wife of Philadelphia are visiting relatives here.

Harry Simpson is visiting his brother George Simpson on Market Street.

Joseph Owens is giving his fence a coat of paint.

August 17

Mr. Sheppard Robbins has been treating himself to a new carriage.

Mr. H. Nicholson's building presents a much better appearance since its removal.

Several Port Norris boats will take part in the race at Fortescue to-morrow. Several of our citizens also will witness the sport at Sea Breeze on that day.

Mr. Westley Hiles and family, of Haleyville, are visiting David T. Robbins.

Mr. William Baker's new house on East Brown Street is enclosed.

Mr. Gus Henry and wife returned home yesterday after a three weeks' trip.

Base ball is raging here. I see the most recent scores having already been published in the *News*.

August 18

Edward Reeves of Harmony and John More of Bridgeton, intend on starting a gents' furnishing store in Port Norris in the near future.

The sloop "Mint," Andrew Hailer captain, is loading with pine wood for Philadelphia.

H. H. Nicholson has moved his wheelwright shop opposite the butcher shop, he is going to enlarge it and keep furniture.

August 19

The base ball nine went to Haleyville Saturday and played a game.

Andrew Vail, a captain of the Elvin English took a party to Fortescue Monday. There were 25 persons on board, the captain, Andrew Vail and wife, two daughters and their poodle, Mrs. Frank Hand and daughter, of Camden, Mrs. Ann Hansel, Mrs. E. Lore, Mrs. L. Kline, Mr. Joe Laws, of Philadelphia, Mrs. Sallie Bowen, Mrs. Lillie Hutten Lock of Dividing Creek, George Sloan, his daughter and two sons, Clarence Gibson, Bertie Lore, Ephraim Haines and family and the butcher, B. H. After dinner Harry Pierson and Lempel Sloan caught some crabs and some clams. They spent five hours at Fortescue and returned home in good time, the sea was running high and after some had fed the sharks they felt better.

Sutton & Harris, our new butchers are doing a good business in Mauricetown. They run over there Wednesdays and Fridays and gather up orders for Saturdays.

Mr. L. Newcomb, general secretary of the Y. M. C. A., of Detroit, who has been visiting friends here returned home yesterday. P.

LAKE – At Port Norris, Aug. 17, 1886, Belle, daughter of John, Jr. and the late Belle Lake, age 10-1/2 months.

August 20

Samuel Shinn, of Port Norris, lost a valuable horse one day last week under very peculiar circumstances. The animal had torn down the partition between the stalls, and stumbled and fell on a pointed post that stood nearby. The post pierced through its side, and made a large hole, through its side, and made a large hole, through which the entrails of the horse protruded and ran out. The animal died in a few minutes.

Captain Lewis Anderson, of the Katie Barton, took a party to Cape May on Wednesday.

A big lot of folks were on the excursion Wednesday. Rather damp coming home.

CAST ASHORE ON AN ISLAND

A PORT NORRIS' MAN FOUR YEARS AMONG A STRANGE PEOPLE

Enforced Life among a race of Japanese
The Characteristics of the People and the Climate of the Country
His Long Silence Accounted for

The following extremely interesting letter has just been received at Port Norris from Charles E. Turner, a former citizen of that place. He had not been heard from by friends or relatives for four years and had almost been given up for lost. He is now residing in Yokahama, Japan, where he first made his home eight years ago. The letter is dated, "Yokahama, Japan, July 22, 1886."

He says: I am enjoying extremely good health, not having had one hour's sickness since first I arrived in this country; weigh 112 lbs, which has been my standing weight for three years.

"Regarding the people of the country I can truly say that never in all my travels have I found such a race of people. They are kind, good hearted, as it is possible for a being to be, and there is no doubt about their being among the first as to intelligence. They are very enterprising in every way and a very proud nation. They are adopting foreign ways and means faster than any nation in the east. The government is more on the Dutch principle than ours, and is ruled by an emperor. The religion throughout the Country is mostly the Mohamet form of worship, except in the cities of Yokahama, Hakodate, Kaba, and Nagasaki, where they have mostly all home

Christian believers and I suppose in time, if the missionaries continue to work in the future as they have in the past, it will be a Christian country throughout.

"I have had considerable experience among another class of people during the last four years whom I do not know what to call, but they are similar to a race called the Inoes. Four years ago the last of this August myself and three other officers of the Mitsu Bishi ships bought and fitted out a schooner for the purpose of otter hunting (which is carried on quite extensively from this port and is very profitable if successful); but soon after we arrived at the islands, which are a small group away up to the northward of the Japan Islands, we encountered a heavy gale and were driven on shore upon a small island. We lost the schooner and all but ourselves and crew, which was very fortunate, as we learned afterward that two other schooners were lost during the same gale and not a member of either seen or heard tell of afterward. We found the people (who were very few, there not being more than a hundred and fifty all told) like all other Japanese in regard to kindness and hospitality. The men are short, thick and very dark, with a white heavy beard and long hair which they never cut. The women are similar as regards to shape, but differ greatly in other respects. The men are as homely as human beings could possibly be while the women are to the other extreme as handsome featured as any I ever saw; the only thing that makes them look bad is a peculiar way they paint themselves, which is a ring around the mouth. They use the juice from a root which they put on, and it turns as black as a coal immediately after administrating. The climate is extremely cold, but we did suffer much through that as we were supplied with good native clothing which is made of bears' skins so that the hair fits on the inside.

The way that we slept was in sort of a bag made of skins, in which two of us would get together, and then lace up on the inside, and there we would be twice as warm as toast. The only houses that they have are small huts built of mud which is plastered on poles that are bent in a half circle and both ends sticking in the ground. The worst thing we had to contend with at first was the food which consisted of fish, venison, bear's meat, herbs and roots, but we soon learned to appreciate it and I think the fare agreed with us all for during that time we all gained considerable flesh.

"Now we were on the island from the 18th of September, 1882 until the 20th of March, 1886: during that time we never saw the sign of a vessel of any description until, on the above date, there came a Japanese whale brig close to the island and some of her crew came ashore to cut some wood and they were kind enough to take us off and landed us at Cladwistock, Russia. From there we got back to Yokahama all right. Now you can understand why you did not hear from me for so long a time."

August 22

We forgot to tell you how many were on our excursion Wednesday. There were about 400; 268 on the early train and the balance on the afternoon train. The cornet brass band of this place was invited and played a tune at the depot at Cedarville and then they went head and all the rest fell in and paraded through Cedarville and back to the grove, playing most of the time. Quite a number of cedarvillians came out and we all had a good time. Several organists and singers of both places did good work.

August 23

A Philadelphia party will be in a few days open a store in what is called the Champion Building.

It is said that A. Ballentine has got the prime late potato patch of the season.

Miss Emma Conover is lying dangerously ill at her home.

Miss Leonora Adams, the daughter of Mr. James R. Adams, is home from Camden for a few days.

Miss Sophia Robinson has been the guest of her cousin, Miss Ella Lake, for a few days recently.

Charles W. Ingersoll has been offered a school at Jefferson to teach the coming season. He will make a good teacher.

The house of Henry Lake is nearly completed and he will take charge of it in a few days.

John Dixson and wife have returned home after a week's visit at Shiloh.

George Robbins is going to build a house on High Street, opposite the first ward school house.

David Bennett and wife have gone home after a week's visit among relatives.

Another boat race Thursday.

Miss Addie Bloxsom and Miss Emma Matthews have gone to Camden for a visit.

Miss Emma Hutchinson left for her home on Saturday.

The colored peoples' camp meeting commenced at Dragston Saturday.

Captain Lewis Anderson, of the Katie Barton took a party to Cape May on Wednesday. He had on board himself and family, Phillip Barber, Charles Broadwater, George Simpson, and family, David S. Bennett and wife, and Harry Simpson, of Philadelphia who is here to visit relatives.

Mr. Samuel Shinn's horse got to kicking Wednesday night and kicked the side of the stall down and fell on a broken plank killing itself.

Mrs. L. L. Newman left here yesterday for Tuckahoe to visit her uncle after which she will leave for her home in Detroit, Michigan.

J. E. Prichard is having a large trade in flour.

Mr. Levi Robbins and family are gone to Pleasant Mount, Pennsylvania, for two weeks visit among their friends.

John Cobb has a new horse and says it is the best in the place. It indulged in a little runaway yesterday, however, and spilled out a lot of potatoes.

August 24

Mr. Charles Whitaker and family returned home Saturday night after a week's trip among friends and relatives.

We hear that Mr. Levi Robbins is very sick; so sick he cannot come home. He and his family went visiting friends at Mount Pleasant, Pennsylvania and he was taken sick the same day he arrived. The lodge has been notified.

We hear that Mr. William Ballenger and family of Mores' Mill, near Bridgeton, talk of moving here if they can find things to suit them.

Doctor Henry C. Fithian and some others are getting up a sloop race for all Maurice River sloops to take place on Thursday next.

Mrs. Mary Hand and daughter returned home from Camden yesterday accompanied by Miss Ada Vail.

Complaint is still made about the Post Office being so far off and not even a small box in the centre of the town.

The Port Norris Knights of Pythias are going to build a new town hall and lodge room. They have not decided yet where to put it as they have two or three sites under consideration. It is to be a Public Hall down stairs and Lodge room up stairs. The specifications are drawn up and will be put out soon.

The Haleyville base ball club came down here Saturday and was wiped up by the Port Norris nine.

August 25

A Flotilla - Port Norris Gala Day

A BIG BOAT RACE TO BE SAILED AT THE OYSTER CITY OVER THE WATERS OF THE FAMOUS COVE.

The people of Port Norris are getting up a big excitement over the boat race to come off at that place on the next Thursday by the sloops owned on the Maurice River. All creation down that way are expecting to be out in the bay, and there is little but that the white sails which will dot this celebrated cove on that day will make a pretty sight. There are three handsome prizes to be sailed for, as follows:

First Prize – a silver pitcher and tray; second prize – a gold and silver card receiver; third prize - a gold lined silver cup.

The following boats have been entered: The Laura May, Johnson, Buzby, Trader, Henry & Howard, William Dennis, Mayflower, R. E. English, Rosa B., Maud M., and Frances R. Lake.

The race will be sailed according to the following plan: Starting at twenty minutes of nine o'clock in the morning at Long Reach, opposite the oyster houses, the boats will sail down and out the mouth of the river, taking the main channel to the eastward of the buoy and to the westward of a boat anchored off the outer point of East point bar; from there around two stake boats to be anchored off in the bay or cove at points to be decided on by the judges on day of race, so that there shall be a boat to windward, one course on the wind and one course with the wind free; the judges to say on the morning of the race where the stake boats shall be placed and how the boats in the race shall round the stake boats, whether to port or starboard. The course to be not less than 25 miles or more than 30 miles; the race to be sailed on time allowance of one minute to the foot. All boats to be measured after the race by putting a plumb line forward of the mast and where the boat takes the water measuring with a tape between said points.

Returning boats shall pass to the westward of the stake boat, off the point bar and to the eastward of buoy and by main channel up the river to the oyster houses to the point of starting. The judges are David Robbins, Leonard Hand, Henry Berry, Major McDaniels, and Edward Stites.

Four weeks ago John W. Cornwell, on retiring, stepped on a needle and broke it off in his foot; he could not work for two weeks and yesterday it hurt him worse. He pressed on it some and the eye part of the needle, about three quarters of an inch long, came out.

Levi Robbins and family have returned home.

Mrs. Frank Howard is quite sick.

Miss Lillie Howard returned home to-day after a week visit at Bridgeton.

P.

August 26

Captain James Matthews' cellar is dug for his new house on High street.

Mr. Sheppard Robbins intends to give a grand party on Friday evening in honor of the boat race.

A few families in Port Norris have spent part of this week making cider. We hope to test the quality before we speak of it.

Mr. Wallie Stites had a son two days ago.

Mr. Joshua Cobb's son Henry nearly cut his hand off yesterday.

A large crowd was at the river yesterday to witness the boat race. There were eleven boats racing and three prizes awarded, the Rosa B., taking 1st, the Dennis, the second, and the Johnson, the third.

Captain Lewis Andrews took Mr. William Brunyate and family and others out fishing the other day and there was a lot of fishing but Miss Francis Terry was the only one that caught a fish and she caught a nice big one. I guess they bite better now.

August 27

The remains of Mrs. Lina Robbins, wife of Warren Robbins, are to
be disinterred and placed by the side of her husband in the
Methodist cemetery in Port Norris. It was Warren's request to lie
together.

He was born at Port Norris, November 7th 1860, and lived there all
his life, till the past year. Four years ago he married Miss Lina
Lake, a lovely Christian lady. The union was a very happy one
until sickness separated them. The second of September 1885 he
went to Colorado on account of lung trouble; his mother went with
him, his wife not being able to go, but promised to join him in the
winter. Six weeks after he left, death claimed his beloved wife. She
died very sudden of heart disease. The news so completely
prostrated him, that his mother had very little hope of his ever
rallying, but by change and travel he began to improve some, so in
three months his mother left him in Denver and returned to her
home and sent another son out to him, but the first of March, he
was taken so much worse his mother went out again to him and
found him low. The doctors all told her it was his lungs and it was
hardly possible for her to get him home, but by slow travel they
arrived home the 25th of April and he seemed to improve slowly
until a week before he died. After his death a post mortem
examination was held, when his lungs and heart were found to be
perfectly sound, his death was caused by chronic pleurisy.

His death is a terrible blow to his parents, it being the first death of
their children. He died a Christian, not fearing death, but spoke of
the sweet rest in Heaven from all his trouble. He was a loving
husband and father, an affectionate son and brother. He leaves two
small children and many kind friends to mourn his loss. He died
the 20th of July at his father's, 65 South Laurel, Bridgeton.

August 28

Perhaps it would be well for me to state that the post office is changed to the opposite side of the street, as a certain man the other night did not know it was changed and went feeling all around for the mailbox in the dark. We wish it was moved more central; not at one end of the street as it is now.

Timothy Bateman has moved into his new house on the corner of Main and High Streets.

The boat race prizes were a silver pitcher, silver cup and a silver card receiver.

Gus Henry and David T. Robbins have put up a nice fence between their property.

We understand that Mr. Edwin M. Ware is thinking of moving to Bridgeton. He will be greatly missed here.

The Red Men had a grand time last night.

Mrs. S. C. Andrews is quite sick.

Mr. Fred Duffield has moved in George Sloan's house.

September 1

The Cohanzick Tribe of Red Men, accompanied by the Cornet Band made a visitation, by invitation, to Idaho Tribe, of Port Norris, last evening. They went down in the regular train at 5 o'clock and returned in a special. The Millville tribe was also present.

September 2

The oyster season opened September 1st, and a number of boats went to work in Maurice River Cove. In a few days oyster shipments over the Cumberland and Maurice River road will begin to be numerous and heavy.

Mr. Williard McDaniels buried his only child yesterday, a little boy, Harry, about two months old.

Reverend Samuel Hann and family returned home on Tuesday after a few days visit here. He preached a good sermon Sunday night at the Baptist church. Those who were not there missed something.

Lizzie Brown is assisting the Post-mistress at present.

September 3

Sutton & Harris, our new butchers, have changed their boarding place from Mrs. E. Lore's to Lemuel Robbins.

Some of the people thought there was another earthquake Thursday night, Mr. Joseph Stanford's platform with about three tons of coal broke down.

September 8

The Port Norris Knights of Pythias Lodge met last Saturday night to decide where to put the new town hall and they decided to put it on Main Street, west of Joseph Onens' lumber yard. Some of them are afraid a town hall will not pay, as some say they only get 2 or 3 dollars an evening for it. We suppose they are thinking of what they use to get for the old school for an evening. Perhaps they have forgotten the experience Miss Lizzie Bacon went through for a Wigwam for an evening to hold her entertainment in. People would expect to pay more for a hall then they do for a school house and there would be more come if there was any place to hold an entertainment in and there would be more gotten up here to.

Mr. John Hignut has purchased a building lot of Leonard Hand on Chestnut Street between Bacon and Church streets and he intend building soon as he can make arrangements with the carpenters.

September 9

Middletown Morsels

Our public schools commenced on Monday under the instruction of Mr. Albert Carlisle, of Mauricetown.

Mr. G. Fisher, of Bridgeton, preached for us on Sunday.

There was a surprise party at Mr. Charles Pepper's last Thursday night.

Mr. Elwood Fisher, our popular shoemaker, has his work in the front part of his residence.

Our hack men are still on the road.

The schooner Polka took a pleasuring party down the river on Tuesday.

September 10

Quite a number intended to drive up from here to the fair but the rain stopped most of them although the rain did not keep all from the cars as some went.

Mr. David Lake is selling out his store goods and is going to rent his house and store. His store would make a first rate place for a barber shop or tobacco store.

Some of the oyster hucksters have stopped buying until it gets cooler. Some of the oystermen have laid up a few days waiting for better prices. We think we ought to have some manufactories here and not have to depend altogether on the oysters. There are many young men with nothing to do but gunning, fishing, &c. Why wouldn't a canning house pay here? Who will be the first to start some enterprising business here? We have a number of stores but not factories, &c. Come on. P.N.

September 11

This weather is bad on the oysters. Several boats went out yesterday and threw their oysters out on the grounds again, several thousand on each boat.

Mr. Charles Harris has moved into his new house on Chestnut Street, and is painting, papering, &c.

Peddlers and peddling wagons are numerous here.

We are glad to learn that Mrs. William Miller is improving.

Masters Bert and Lucien Ware are enjoying the society of their little friends in Bridgeton this week.

September 13

Mr. Richard Stites has the stakes driven for his new house on North Market Street.

Enoch Danzenbaker was found dead in his little house at Long Reach yesterday afternoon. He was about 70 years of age and almost a stranger here.

Miss Emma Conahay has been quite sick with typhoid fever.

Miss Mattie Magee is so much better as to be able to be out again.

September 15

Mr. S. Irvin Middleton, proprietor of the River Hotel at Port Norris, has been making extensive improvements in his hostelry. New floor, fresh paint and paper have added much to the interior of the building, so that it is now one of the neatest and most pleasant hotels in South Jersey.

September 16

Quite a number went to Dividing Creek to the Baptist Association yesterday and they report having a very pleasant time.

Miss Emma Lake is improving slowly.

Miss Sylvia Vale is quite sick.

Mrs. Braiman, of Philadelphia, and others are visiting Captain Andrew Vail's.

We hear that David Lake has rented his store.

We have the same school teachers this year as last. They must have given us satisfaction. There are four of them – Mr. Theodore Fleetwood, principal, Mr. Campbell, Mr. Hand and Miss Carson.

FOUND DEAD IN HIS CABIN

SUDDEN PASSING AWAY OF ENOCH DANZENBAKER, OF LONG REACH

The Sad night That Met the Gaze of Some Neighbors
Blow- flies Buzz a Death Song
Mr. Danzenbaker's Long Life and Retiring Nature

Just across the railroad at Long Reach, below Port Norris, stands a little cabin, one-story and cheerless, in which has lived alone for the last six months Enoch Danzenbaker.

About the middle of yesterday afternoon some neighbors had their attention aroused by a large number of blow-flies about the window of the cabin and it occurred to them to look in and see what the cause of it was.

The object that met their gaze was the body of the aged inhabitant of the cabin, lying upon his bed, dead. His clothing was on, his boots off. One hand grasped firmly a package of crackers; the other held tightly to some cheese. The blow flies in large numbers were hovering noisily around their sickening feast. Medical aid was at once summoned in the person of Doctor Stetson Bacon, but Enoch Danzenbaker was far beyond the reach of human skill, and nothing could be done beyond making the remains as cleanly and orderly as possible, in preparation for the time when they should be given their last resting place. The doctor thought that the death had occurred in a fit. Undertaker Auld, of Dividing Creek, took charge of the body.

The deceased was but little known in the neighborhood where he died, having been neutrality of a retiring disposition, and having had but little to do with those by whom he was surrounded. Since last Friday he had not been seen until the hour when found dead in bed, and just when death took place does not seem to be clear. Probably it had been some time before, however, for a while a large, powerfully built man, the body was swollen far beyond its normal condition.

Enoch Danzenbaker was always a peculiar man in his nature, and always lived a retiring, saving life. He has never, until recently at least, travelled any, and although about seventy remarked last spring that as he had never seen Philadelphia he thought he should have to make a trip there.

He was born on a farm just west of Null's Mill, which he afterwards inherited and where he had always resided until last spring. When about 50 he married a Miss Reed, who died some time ago, leaving him with one daughter. The farm was a large one, and owing to his economical habits it was supposed that he was fairly well to do. This was the case; we are informed, until his marriage, which seems to have been an unfortunate one. Then things began to go backward and last spring the farm was sold from him. His daughter went to live with a family at Fries burg and he went to Long Reach and took up his lonely residence in the little cabin.

Since going to Long Reach he had worked in the boats a little and it is reported that a little money of his was held for him by different parties, but his unfortunate circumstances and domestic troubles had doubtless much to do with his death. The late Mrs. Noah Johnson, of Friesburg, was a half sister of his and the late Daniel Danzenbaker was a cousin. A few relatives are now living.

September 20

Work has begun on the new bridge across the run west of the house of George Robbins, Sr. we hope it will be high enough not to stop travel in a full tide, as it has done before.

Mr. H. Nicholson, the undertaker, is having his place of business enlarged to twice its former size. We understand he intends on laying in a stock of furniture.

Mr. Stephen R. Mayhew intends to put a set of scales in front of his establishment.

Mr. S. Irwin Middleton, the hotel keeper, is having a barber shop built in his side yard, next to the railroad.

SCRIBBLER

September 21

Freeholder Thomas Hand and road overseer Levi Lore are progressing rapidly with the new bridge over Robbins' run. It is to be 58 feet long and 12 feet wide in the clear and will be a very fine bridge, - just what is needed.

Mr. D. Sharp of Bridgeton has the cellar dug for his new house on East Main Street.

P.

September 22

Knights of the Mystic Chain

The Select Castle, Ancient Order Knights of the Mystic Chain of New Jersey, will meet in annual session at Port Norris this morning at ten o'clock and will continue for two or three days. A large representation from the different castle throughout the state will be present. A number of the supreme officers of the supreme castle and delegation from the select castles of Pennsylvania, Delaware and Maryland are expected to be present. The mark degree will be conferred on all past commanders of the state and a large amount of accumulated business for the past year will be disposed of.

Mr. Amos Pepper's and Mr. James Matthew's new house are both raised.

Mr. Haines, Sr., has moved in his new house on North Bacon Street, and Mr. George Lucas moved yesterday into the house vacated by Mr. Haines.

Captain Everett Hollinger and wife have gone to housekeeping in part of Henry Ayer's house.

Mr. John Chew and wife are going to housekeeping in part of Mr. Chew's home on east Main Street.

Mr. William Fowler, Sr., has been improving appearance of his property by a new fence.

Business was dull at Long Reach yesterday.

September 23

Mr. Ayer Moore has another fine daughter. We are sorry to say he talks of moving to Elmer about the first of next month if he can sell his house, and if not I believe he will rent it as he wants to go.

Reverend Mr. Scott, of Greenwich, is to give a temperance lecture here on Saturday evening. He will also fill Reverend Mr. Lorenzo Appleby's pulpit on Sunday in the Baptist church.

This cool weather makes folks think about quilting. There was a quilting party of Mrs. David Hallinger's [**Hollinger**] yesterday. No doubt we will have more.

September 26

A carpet rag sewing was held at Mrs. Oliver Webb's on Thursday last.

Mr. Benjamin Campbell has rented Mr. David Lake's store.

Mr. David T. Robbins is having his store cleaned this week, getting ready for his fall goods.

Mr. Harrison Fleetwood moved yesterday to Dividing Creek.

Mr. G. J. Michael a salesman from M. Merregan, of Philadelphia lost his pocketbook yesterday. It had about $5.00 cash and $120.00 in checks. He says the finder may have the cash if he returns the checks. He says a bank is needed here. He had to telegraph for money to get away with.

September 27

Mr. John Hignut moved over in Berrytown last Saturday and Mr. Atiles moved in Robbinstown, in Mr. Blackman's house.

On Sunday morning Mr. Aquilla Miller was presented with a fine daughter.

Mrs. Sylvia Vail and Miss Emma Conahay are improving very fast, we are glad to say, but Emma Lake has not been so well.

Markets are better now. That is pretty good for good oysters.

September 30

Mr. Benjamin Campbell went to Philadelphia Tuesday to lay in his store goods as he is to take charge of David Lake's store October 1st. We wish him success.

Work on the new bridge is still going on and it looks as though it would be a substantial one when done.

Can't the young fellows be punished for stealing flowers? There is a good bit of complaint about their stealing tuberoses and other flowers.

All citizens wishing their mail brought up to David T. Robbins' store can have it brought free of charge or delivered for one cent (providing they do not live too far off) by Charles B. Robbins, Jr. he will also mail any left there free. This is quite a convenience and ought to be appreciated, as the post office is way off at one end of the town and not even a letter box elsewhere.

October 6

Fire at Port Norris

On last Saturday night the house of Mr. Thomas Hand, Port Norris, caught fire while the family, were all out. A lamp which had been left on the table exploded lighting the furniture in the room, fortunately Mr. Hand returned before the fire had time to spread beyond the room, which prevented a more serious fire.

October 8

Captain Andrew Vail, on his way from town last week, anchored near Chester, when he hove his anchor up caught something on his chain, very heavy, which proved to be an anchor weighing about 1500 pounds.

Mr. E. J. Cook is building is a new porch on the rear of his house.

Mrs. David T. Robbins is going to have her fall and winter opening on Saturday next. Now for new styles, she has lots of hats, bonnets, &c.

October 11

An oyster schooner was run into by a tug in the Maurice River one day last week and sunk.

Three gentlemen at Port Norris, William Fowler, William Pepper and Henry Berry, sat as a board of arbitrators on Monday to decide whether Mr. Richard Lore, of Newport, or Mr. Silas Robinson, of Dividing Creek have the better right to certain oyster grounds in the bay, decision reserved until at one o'clock. Each of the disputants bound themselves in the sum of $300 to abide by the decision. Twenty-six witnesses were examined.

October 12

Reverend A. Hodder, former pastor of the Baptist church, was here on Sunday and preached both morning and evening in said church.

Old Mrs. Rachel Trader, mother of Hester Mulford, had a stroke of the palsy on Saturday last, and has not spoken or swallowed since she was found out in the yard by one of the neighbors.

Richard Stites' new house is enclosed.

If the weather proves fine, there is quite a number going to the convention on Wednesday to Newport from here. JUMBO

October 13

The house of Thomas Hand Sr., in Port Norris was the scene of excitement on Saturday night last. It appears that when Mr. Hand went to bed, as usual he left a lamp burning on the table. He retired about nine o'clock and at eleven a young lady went into the room and discovered that the lamp had burst and set fire to the room. The flames had burned a hole about eight feet in diameter in the partition and a small hole through the ceiling. The young lady quickly gave notice and several young people who were attending a party commenced to extinguish the flames which they soon had under control. A few minutes later and the entire building would have been in a blaze and it happened just near the pump so all the water would have been shut off. As it is it will take several dollars to repair the damage, but the building is saved.

October 12

MIDNIGHT MARAUDERS AT PORT NORRIS

Five Masked Men Attempt to Break into Houses, and One is Shot

About one o'clock this morning a man was shot while attempting to break into the house of Frazier Gland which is situated half way between Port Norris and Dividing Creek. Mr. Gland is an old man and lives in this house with his sister Ruth Gland and his nephew Henry Lore. At midnight they were all three aroused by mysterious noises made by attempts to enter the house. It has been generally understood that Mr. Gland has some money hidden in his house and robberies have been feared, and for some time Mr. Gland has been, as he was this time, fully prepared to give visitors a warm reception. So when the would-be-robbers made their demands they were answered by a volley from Harry Lore's shot gun. Five men, masked and blackened then started to run away when one of them fell, shot, but was quickly picked up and carried off. The marauders have not yet been identified but it is thought they will soon be cared for by Sheriff Williams. It is possible some of the young men in that neighborhood know more of this escapade than they now wish to tell the public. It seems that at 10 o'clock Captain Richard Buckaloo and Mrs. Burnight, whose families occupy a double house just out of Port Norris, in the direction of Gland's, were aroused by parties outside, when the Captain opened his window and cried out that he knew the visitors and the five men who were masked took to their heels at a lively rate. At one o'clock Mrs. Burnight was again aroused by these fellows returning, and they broke up a stove and other furniture that was in an out-kitchen. She could distinguish three men in this last party and one was limping badly. The neighborhood is much excited and they are determined to find out whether these men was drunken rowdies or desperate robbers and in either case these fellows will probably get a taste of Jersey justice.

October 15

We thinks "Reed's Hall, Port Norris," in a recent issue of the *News,* should have been "Elmer."

Misses Mattie and Janie Robbins have begun dress making in the rear of Benjamin Campbell's store.

The new bridge is nearly done and looks first rate. It is wide enough for a side walk both sides of it.

P.N.

October 16

Mr. Abbott, of Bridgeton, moved this week in part of John Broadwater's house on South Bacon Street. He is going to move in one of George Robbins' new houses as soon as they are completed.

Mr. William McDaniels has moved in part of James D. Cobb's house.

While the constable was down at the river one day this week a certain young man down there thought he would have some fun by getting him to put the handcuffs on him and walk up in that form. While he was gone his partner thought he was arrested and hired a man in his place. Now who got fooled?

P.N.

October 17

Harry Pierson goes to Port Norris to-morrow to spend a few days.

Moore and Reeve have a very pretty establishment at Port Norris near the station and are doing a driving trade. The young gentlemen richly deserve success and is receiving it.

Joseph Torrell, of Port Norris, spent Sunday in Bridgeton.

Miss Phebe Parsons, who has been spending a few days with friends in Bridgeton, returns to her house at Port Norris today.

A party of deer hunters started from Port Norris yesterday. It consisted of Jacob Leiber, Constant Hand, and James Garrison. They will eat a deer, it is whispered, if they have to buy one!

October 18

Messrs. Gardiner and George S. Senser are to speak in the old protestant church on Tuesday evening. All are invited to hear them.

A "Tin Wedding" made a merry evening to many on Saturday. Mr. and Mrs. Jack O'Brien were the lucky recipients, having been married just ten years.

A "Variety Wedding" takes place at Mrs. Enoch Sharp's to-night, by way of celebrating their twelve years of married life. Next!

Mr. George Fisk has left John Cobb's and gone to board with Mrs. David Hallinger [**Hollinger**].

Mr. David T. Robbins has had his signs brightened by the painter's brush, giving them a much neater appearance. P.N.

October 20

General Clinton Bowen Fisk is to give a lecture here next Saturday night.

Mr. Thomas Rogers and family, who live at Long Reach, are going to move to Camden, where they came from, in a few days. Mr. Elwood Fisher, from Cedarville, is going to go where Mr. Rogers moves from.

There was a big time last night at Daniel Garrison's. They collected $32 for his lame son, James, who lives at Haleyville, and gave him a suit and his wife a dress. Someone went after them and brought them home.

P.N.

October 21

Four moving yesterday. Mr. William Hand and family moved in Captain Vale's house. Mr. George Everingham moved where Hand vacated. Mr. John Dillahay of Goshen, father of Samuel Dillahay, moved where Mr. Everingham vacated. Mr. Edwin M. Ware moved in David Lake's house, corner Main and Markets streets.

Mr. David T. Robbins has just been getting in another lot of new wall papers, oil cloths, &c.

Miss Hulda Fleetwood rides out on pleasant days. She has been to Millville, and many are anxious to see her at the lecture on Saturday of this week.

October 22

Mr. E. J. Cook, the popular clothing dealer of Port Norris was in Bridgeton yesterday. Mr. Cook is one of the leaders of the Knights of Pythias there. He examined the handsome new Estey organ which is to be given away Christmas (as the purchasers of the *Favorite* decide), and was greatly pleased with the instrument. The Knights of Port Norris are after the prizes and purposes "getting there" or very near it.

The new bridge is about done and looks well. It has three railings and we think it will be sufficient for the big tides.

Several small houses are being built at Long Reach. Two families are going to move down there from Bridgeton this week.

House keeping is very fashionable at present, and the house wives are very busy.

Mr. Thomas Hallinger [**Hollinger**] has the cellar dug for a new house on North Market Street. Mr. George Belford is going to take Mr. H.'s present house as soon as the latter vacates. P.N.

October 24

There is a family by the name of Glann living a couple of miles out of Port Norris that have long been noted for their eccentricity and recluse habits. For a number of years they have lived almost exclusively by themselves rarely frequenting the town, and the present head of the family, Frazier Glann, hasn't been in town (Port Norris) for some seventeen years. A rumor was current in the village this morning that a party of five men visited their house at 12 midnight last night, and that one of their number was shot by a nephew staying with the family and carried off by the other four, but we give it only as rumor, the fact not being vouched for.

October 25

The prohibition meeting was largely attended Saturday night.

General Clinton B. Fisk and Reverend T. L. Gardiner spent Sunday with us. Reverend Doctor T. L. Gardiner preached in the Baptist church in the morning, and General Fisk followed, touching on very good points. The latter also addressed the Sunday school. The Methodist church is being frescoed and consequently they had no service and the Baptist was well attended. Maybe wish the general to come again.

The Baptist church was crowded on Sunday, in union with the Methodist people, when General Fisk again spoke, taking for his theme the Sunday school lesson of the day. After a pleasant little speech before the Sunday school in the afternoon he left us, and will make a short stay at Mauricetown, the other gentleman going to Bridgeton. The visit has been much enjoyed by us and will not soon be forgotten.

About forty oystermen, who arrived in the river late and were anxious to reach their homes by the regular 6:45 train from Port Norris, were much disappointed to find that the train did not leave until 10 pm to allow a company of excursionists to attend the political meeting. All sorts of reflections were cast at the agent and conductor who, however, had nothing to do with the arrangements of the train. The conclusion arrived at, was that the public should have timely notice of such changes that great inconvenience may be avoided.

October 26

Mr. Editor

The "Band of Hope" is going to give an entertainment in the Baptist Church next Saturday evening. All are invited.

Quite a number of persons were out to hear General Clinton Bowen Fisk Saturday evening.

A couple of young ladies of this place got lost we suppose or bewildered one night last week. When they were found it was discovered that they were in a huge iron pipe, near the new bridge. It was soon found that one of them was fast and it took considerable time and energy for the other to release her, but by strong pulling and hard pushing she was at last set free.

Hallow-E'en

Hallow even or Hallowe'en is the name popularly given to the eve or vigil of All Hallows, or festival of All Saints which, being the 1st of November. Hallowe'en is the evening of 31st of October. As this falls on Sunday next, Saturday night will be observed by the boys and girls as All Hallowe'en. In England it was customary to crack nuts, duck for apples in a tub of water, and perform other harmless fireside revelries. While the same thing can be said of Scotland, the Hallowe'en ceremonies of that country partook more of a superstitious character; taking, among rustics, the form of a charm to discover who should be his or her partner for life. Of these now almost exploded customs, the best summary is that contained in Burn's poem "Hallowe'en."

October 27

ROUSING MEETING OF PROHIBITIONISTS

Smith Gardiner and General Clinton Bowen Fisk, sided by the Fisk Glee Club appear before a large Meeting at the Oyster City.

The people of Port Norris turned out in large numbers on Saturday evening to welcome General Fisk, the prohibition candidate for Governor. An excursion train went from this city which carried about 200 persons down from here; it was estimated that there were nearly 1000 people to listen to the addresses. The Port Norris Brass band furnished music and the Fisk Glee Club of this city gave several songs their best style.

The speaking was from the portico of the residence of Mr. George Onens, the meeting being in the open air. The first speaker was Mr. Frank C. Smith of New York, who was followed by Reverend T. L. Gardiner, of Shiloh, the candidate for Senator on the Prohibition ticket.

General Clinton Bowen Fisk made the last speech, which was one of the best, and it was most enthusiastically received by the last audience.

The excursionists returned home at the close of the meeting, the train arriving up about 11 o'clock.

October 28

The little Band of Hope is to have an entertainment on Saturday night next, all are invited.

The cellar is dug for another new house on North Bacon Street.

Mr. Nichols is to speak here on Saturday night next. Many want to hear General Clinton Bowen Fisk again. Some were away and did not hear him.

The Fisk Glee Club of Port Norris Saturday night were entertained at supper by Captain Bloxsom and are loud in their praises of the Captain's hospitality.

Mr. B. F. Horner sent one of his popular New Home sewing machines here yesterday for demonstration to the ladies.

October 29

Quite a number of ladies went from here to Mrs. Ruth Comer's, at Haleyville, yesterday on a quilting party and they report a good time.

Mr. Richard Stites' new house is near completion and as soon as it is done Mr. Eugene Roley and family are to move where he vacates.

Mr. Theodore Fleetwood has been sick these last two days, consequently no school in his department.

November 1

On Sunday afternoon Mr. Theophilus Newcomb was presented with a fine dishwasher.

On account of the weather on Saturday night the Band of Hope and ladies of the W. C. T. U. put off their entertainment until Sunday night and they had a very good one. It was in the Baptist church and it was crowded. A silver collection was taken up, which was a liberal one, to defray the expenses of the band of Hope and W. C. T. U.

November 2

Some think the election should be here instead of Haleyville as the majority of the men are here. Even from surrounding towns it would save considerable carting.

Mr. Joseph Onens is having his office enlarged, also a portico in front of it.

Mr. Lorenzo Burnite is moving where John Hignut vacated.

Mr. John Cobb says his hay was worth $180. That was he had 18 stacks, his whole summer's work, burned Monday. Too bad!

November 3

Several shippers in Port Norris are sending from 100 to 150 sacks of oysters to Philadelphia daily.

Bridgeton has 58 telephones subscribers while Millville has but four and Vineland six. Port Norris has seven subscribers, Salem has two, and Cedarville and Fairton have one each.

November 4

Sixteen haystacks belonging to John Cobb, of Port Norris, were burned yesterday afternoon. It is thought they were accidentally set on fire by Mr. Cobb's child and the child of brother, while playing. Owing to the vigilance of those fighting the flames no buildings were burned.

The Republican meeting at Port Norris Saturday night was addressed by lawyer Joslins, of Camden, and Senator Nichols, Colonel Gibson didn't put in an appearance. Little enthusiasm was manifested, and, as we are informed from Port Norris, the meeting wasn't as big as the posters.

November 5

Mr. Samuel Fagan has bought the house now occupied by Mr. James Mathews, and as soon as the latter moves, the former is going to rebuild the house, and then move himself.

Mrs. David T. Robbins has the agency for the Universal Fashion Company, also has fashion books for sale, and can supply all patterns at list prices, and to fit where the measure is taken.

Captain Andrew Vale and others have been taking the quilts this week.

Mrs. Rhoda Hollinger and Mrs. Mary Terry drove over to Millville to-day.

Mrs. Elizabeth Whitaker, from Newport, is visiting friends here.

November 6

Mr. Theodore Moncrief moved here yesterday from Newport in one part of Samuel Carlls' house on North Market Street.

Mr. William Donnelly is building a new house at Long Reach in which he expects to move soon with his family.

"Mourning for Gardiner and Foster," and a piece of crape were the decorations over one of our citizen's door just after election.

Workmen are at work on engine number two, of Cumberland and Maurice River Railroad, repairing furnace, we understand.

James Sutton of the firm Sutton & Harris, butchers of this place, lost his pocketbook while out peddling. It contained $31.

Sutton & Harris will have a new wagon on our streets about the first of next month.

We hear Mrs. H. L. Douglas, of Bridgeton, talks of starting a millinery store here.

Mr. Dory Moncrief of Newport, has moved in part of the house with Than. Lore.

Oysters markets are very poor.

Mr. Sheppard Campbell and Della Shaw, of Newport, spent Thursday with Robert L. Lake and wife.

At the entertainment of the Band of Hope held Sunday evening $11.52 collection was taken up.

November 8

Surprise Party

Talk about your surprise parties, the one at Mr. Warrington L. Hand's caps the climax. To-day being his wife's thirty-fifth birthday he had a host of friends invited who dropped in about 8 o'clock, numbering about sixty, to spend the evening. The evening was spent in playing by the young folks and talking by the old folks until 10:30 pm, when they were called out to take refreshments, and the way that table did groan under its heavy weight of ice cream, cake, bananas, oranges, &c, is a caution. After doing ample justice to the refreshments the company departed wishing Mrs. Hand many more happy birthdays. The barber was the champion eater of the evening. One young man of the company seemed to take a liking to all of the babies.

November 9

The Methodist Episcopal Church looks very pretty with its new coat of frescoing. We are informed that Mrs. Gillie R. Lake, deceased, left them a sum of money to pay for it. Her name, age &c, have been neatly lettered close to the pulpit. There is also more lettering.

Miss Mary Kirby, of Bridgeton, is spending a few days with Miss Nellie Ware.

Mr. Isaac Reeve moved yesterday in one of George Robbins' new houses. We understand the other is now for rent.

We hope this cool weather will help the market and oysters.

November 10

Yesterday afternoon's oyster train from Port Norris contained twenty four cars.

Oysters are getting better all the time. Captain Brown shipped a car load to his customers Saturday from Long Reach.

A great many oystermen who came down on the "owl train" Saturday night were disappointed at having to walk down in the rain. No hack or busses being at the station.

Mrs. William O. Lambert, of Port Norris, is visiting her sister, Mrs. Jeremiah Hann.

November 15

Mr. David Lake is carting lumber to-day for a barber shop on the lot in the rear of Benjamin Campbell's store.

Fred Duffield has moved in part of George Sloan's double house, and a party moved where they vacated, from a distance.

Mr. Charles Harris is enclosing his portico.

Mr. John Cobb is going to have a vendue on Saturday next.

There is a good chance for persons from a distance to get houses here now as several are empty. It is the first time this has been the case for a good while.

Oystermen are doing poor this year.

November 16

Twenty four car loads of oysters were shipped from Long Reach to Philadelphia yesterday afternoon.

Mack Ewing had so many oysters to ship from Long Reach yesterday that several thousand were left on the wharf when the train started at 12 o'clock.

It is stated by the oystermen that at least one third of the oyster boats now working will be laid up inside of a month. This is owing to their oysters being in such a poor condition.

A communication from Port Norris, with a request to publish, informs me that the party at Miss Campbell's, at that place, Wednesday evening of last week, was not invited by her, as announced, but by two young men who were present.

Miss Nellie S. Ware, of Port Norris, spent last night with friends in Bridgeton and acted as an aid at the Japanese supper at the Episcopal Church.

Captain David Hallinger [**Hollinger**] who ran the steamer "Morris" from Bridgeton to Sea Breeze, summer before last, has bought a half interest in the tug "Emma" for $2,500, and is engaged in towing car floats for Baltimore & Ohio Railroad.

Mrs. R. Godfrey, of Philadelphia and Miss Lillian Leslie, of Oswego, N.Y., have been guests of Mrs. Samuel Shinn, at Port Norris.

Reverend Lorenzo G. Appleby preached a sermon to the Red Men in the Baptist church at Port Norris last night.

November 17

A young man of Port Norris tried to enter the store of Warrington L. Hand early Friday morning. He, having another fellow outside to watch, at first tried the shutters, and not succeeding went for the door. About that time, thinking no one was around; out popped a man from the inside. Talk about your clean running, they fairly sailed. But one was captured and was made to confess, and had it not been for their sincere begging and being so young they would have been handled severely for it.

Doctor Stetson L. Bacon of Port Norris, Overseer of the Poor, is paying a visit to the Alms House to-day, to take Rachel Trader, who is over ninety years old. Rachel Trader, an old lady, 90 years of age was brought from Port Norris yesterday and taken to the Alms House.

An Aged Inmate for the Almshouse

An old lady from Port Norris by the name of Rachel Trader was brought up to-day on the Cumberland and Maurice River railroad and taken to the Almshouse. She is over 90 years of age and paralyzed and lay on the floor of the baggage car in an apparently unconscious condition. The neighbors procured an order for her removal last spring but hesitating to send so old a person to the Almshouse have been caring for her through the summer. Now that cold weather was drawing on, however, it was deemed best to send her. We understand that she has a daughter and step son living at Port Norris.

November 18

The Methodist Episcopal Church has been frescoed; it has these words in gold over the choir stand: "Sing to the Lord;" over the pulpit is "Holiness becometh thine house, O Lord, forever," and along side of the pulpit is painted a piece of marble with these words: "In Memoriam, Gillie R. Lake, born September 1st, 1864: died August 1st, 1886." The money was left by her to do the work when she died.

H. H. Nicholson is receiving furniture now for his new business. He opens Saturday, November 20th, with a full line of furniture.

It cost John C. Hand one dollar to play with a dog at the hotel the other day. He threw a silver dollar for Mr. S. Irvin Middleton's dog to bring to him; the dog went to seize a better hold of it and it flew down his throat. If he had paid the dog's tax it would have cost only half that much.

Conductor Howard served a notice from the Cumberland and Maurice River Railroad authorities on John Hollinger to vacate the railroad premises inside of 30 days.

Reverend Mr. Lorenzo Appleby has two more Sundays here yet. His resignation takes effect on the 28th of this month.

A host of friends gathered at Mrs. Robert C. Lore's on Monday and also Tuesday evenings, to help Mrs. Lore sew carpet rags, after which they made the cake and lemonade suffer, returning home about 10:30 o'clock.

Mr. Edward Stites is putting an iron fence in front of his residence.

November 19

A party of young people spent an enjoyable evening with Miss Carrie Campbell last Thursday evening. The party was made up of the following persons: Misses Mellie Chambers, Roxie Corson, Lizzie Pashley, Eva Mayhew, Anna Fowler, Dannie Hoffman, Rettie Eherison. Messrs. H. H. Nicholson, Samuel Meredith, Belford Harris, William Ficken, Seward Sheppard, Edward E. Reeves, Edward Jamison, Bert Pettit and Asher Robbins. After the evening was spent playing games, &c, they helped themselves to the refreshments, all returning home about 12 o'clock, all satisfied with the evening spent.

David R. Lake's barber shop has been raised and nearly enclosed.

John Hollinger has packed his goods and is going to move to Gloucester.

Only seven attended the W. C. T. U. meeting yesterday afternoon. Try and get out next Thursday afternoon at 2:30 o'clock.

No deers for the "dear" party yet. This is the second hunt this season.

Jacob Liber's chimney blowed down night before last.

The oyster train from here cannot make connections satisfactory by leaving the wharf at 2 o'clock, so they are going back to the old time (12 o'clock) to-day for the first.

Reverend Lorenzo G. Appleby preached a very good sermon to the Red Men of this place Sunday evening last, at the Baptist church. The text was from Proverbs 27:28.

November 20

Mrs. Eva Ludlam has been quite sick for a few days, but at this writing she is reported better.

Mr. William Connell, of Philadelphia, has recently moved in James Garrison's house.

Mrs. E. F. Shinn returned from a three weeks visit at Dividing Creek Friday. Mrs. Mary Clark has just returned from a two week visit at Philadelphia, Pedricktown, &c.

One of the prominent features of the coming entertainment will be the exhibition and reading of the first copy of the *Haleyville Item,* a paper which is of home talent and will make many spicy hits.

Mr. Milton Robbins was disappointed in his house at Port Norris and will not move. RAY

November 22

Mr. Richard Stites, moved to-day into his new house on North Market Street.

Mrs. David T. Robbins received a large lot of dress goods &c., to-day.

Mr. Keisle Whitaker of Philadelphia is paying visits among his friends here.

Mr. David R. Lake is raising his barber shop to-day.

Mr. Seth Tribbett is putting up his foundation to-day for his new house.

Mr. William Brunyate and family went to Bridgeton Thursday morning.

November 24

Mrs. Rachel Trader, who was taken from Port Norris to the Almshouse on Wednesday last, died soon after reaching that institution. She was over 90 years of age and paralyzed and it was evident at the time of her arrival that she had not many hours to live.

Mr. James Matthews has moved in his new house on North High Street. Mr. Samuel Fagan, who owns the house that Mr. Matthews vacated, has had the back part torn away with the intention of building a bay window and a new back two stories high. It will be very nice when done.

Mrs. Seth Tribbett has purchased a building lot on South Railroad Avenue of Mr. Thomas Hand at $200, and has a cellar dug for a new house.

Mr. Daniel Sharp's large double house is getting its finishing touches and it is very large and convenient. We hear it is to be occupied by Mrs. Parsons and sons.

Mr. Eugene Roley moved Thursday in the house vacated by Richard Stites on South High Street.

We hear markets for oysters are better now in Philadelphia. We hope it will continue.

A family moved from Cedarville down to Long reach this week.

Mr. Charles Terry moved Thursday in the house vacated by Isaac Reeves.

Mr. Elwood Reeves and Mr. Samuel Shinn were in Bridgeton Tuesday.

Mrs. David T. Robbins was in Philadelphia on Thursday purchasing winter millinery, dry goods, and trimmings.

November 25

A neat, substantial frame building is being erected in the rear of Benjamin Campbell's store, which is to be occupied by Charles Pinkard, of Mauricetown, the well know house and sign painter.

Last week there was quite a gathering of people at the shipyard on the Maurice River, near Long Reach, to witness the launching of the new oyster sloop "I.T. Nichols." Named in honor of Senator Nichols, and just built by Mr. William Parsons, the ship-wright. The vessel went off gracefully, and now lies in the waters of the river, so that in a few days she will be ready for work in the Cove. The "I.T.N." is thirty-one feet keel, and will carry about fifteen tons. She will be commanded by Captain William T. Collins. The owners are William T. Collins, Henry S. Robbins, Leonard C. Hand. The new vessel is handsomely painted. And no prettier sloop or neater model ever sailed out of Maurice River.

A terrible gale of wind accompanied by a fierce rain storm prevailed along the river and in the bay and Cove during a portion of Thursday morning. It lasted about an hour. At Long Reach, several oyster floats were blown from their moorings, and piling along the wharves of the oyster houses were badly damaged. During the gale Captain Walter Fisher, of the schooner "Messenger," met with the rubbers. He was down in the Cove when the storm struck him, and he found himself in a tight box. His anchor chain gave way, and the anchor was lost. He finally came up the river with a three reefed mainsail and bonnet out of his jib. The Captain says that it was a terrible experience, and he doesn't want to go through it again. The wind was so fierce that the situation is likened to that produced by the gale and storm of 1876. It is feared that many of the planted oysters in the Cove have been damaged.

November 26

Mr. Lorenzo Applebee preaches his farewell sermon next Sunday, the 28th.

Mr. Simon moved back to Camden Tuesday where he came from about one year ago, and Mrs. Benjamin Campbell has rented the house he vacated.

Mr. John Cobb has his house keeper back again.

The ladies talk of a fair to be held during the holidays.

The Baptist appointed a committee last Sunday to ascertain what would suit best to have going on Christmas, as the children expect something a little extra then.

Mr. Theophilus Newcomb is carrying his hand in a sling.

JUMBO

November 27

Mr. Richard Stites is a happy man. It's a boy!

A party of young folks spent a pleasant evening last Friday at Miss Carrie Bateman's. It was a masquerade and surprise party. Most of them were dressed in the oddest suits and oldest fashion that was possible. Miss Carrie knew nothing of their coming. She had just arrived home on the train from her school at Bridgeton.

Mr. Walter Peterson's new house is raised.

SUBSCRIBER

Party at Port Norris

Mr. and Mrs. James Mulvey were taken by surprise last evening by a number of young ladies of Mrs. Mulvey's Saturday school class, who called to spend the evening and remind her that it was the anniversary of her birthday. The evening was spent playing various games, singing, &c. Before the party dispersed an old bachelor who was present and had been crossed in love a number of times, suggested that they form a society and agree not any of them to marry for one year and meet again on her next birthday. But the ladies could not see it and suggested that it be decided by vote. The old bachelor after considerable argument came to the conclusion that the suggestion was a good one, and a vote was taken resulting in 1 vote favoring the bachelor's suggestion, which of course, was his own. They presented Mrs. Mulvey with a silver cake basket, the bachelor making the presentation speech.

Port Norris oyster freights have not been very heavy for the past few days, owing to the storm of Thursday last. The season's work thus far has not been very profitable, oysters being as a rule in a poor condition. It is expected the crop will improve later on.

December 1

S. Irwin Middleton, mime host of the Port Norris hotel, has the finest Irish setter in the county.

Some of our Bridgeton sporting men attended the Saturday afternoon shooting match at Port Norris.

Thirty cars, most of which were loaded with oysters, left Long Reach the other day for Philadelphia.

Miss Lenora Sloan is visiting Major Henry Pierson, on Bank Street in Bridgeton.

Mr. J. Woodworth and family arrived home last evening, after spending several days among friends at Deerfield.

On Friday morning last while the schooner "Julia B." was working in the Cove, one of the crew, Stultz Berry, met with a severe accident. In jibing the boat a block strap parted, striking Mr. Berry on the head, making an ugly wound.

Mr. Joseph Sheppard, of Fairton, student at the South Jersey Institute, will preach at the Alms House Sunday afternoon next at three o'clock.

December 2

The fine new sloop, "I.T. Nichols," will soon be in readiness for the oyster business. Joseph S. Turner furnished her with as complete a set of winders and dredges as was ever placed in an oyster vessel. Mr. Turner is a good workman, and understands his business thoroughly.

On Friday evening last a masquerade party numbering about fifty persons, gathered at the residence of Miss Carrie Bateman, and spent a very pleasant evening. Ice cream and other refreshments were served. Some of the costumes were unique and grotesque.

A shooting match took place Saturday afternoon on Freeholder Thomas Hand's lot. The winners were Asher and Guyan Robbins.

Our enterprising barber, Captain Hinson, is doing a rushing business. If you want a good shave give him a call.

When in town go to Elmer Green's for an oyster stew. He knows how to get them up.

December 3

It is a pretty cold day when there is no news at Port Norris. (I mean when there is nothing new to report; we always have the *NEWS*) and today it is somewhat chilly.

You noted in a former paper the resignation of the Reverend Mr. Lorenzo Appleby, pastor of the Baptist church, and last Sunday he preached his farewell sermon. Next Sunday Reverend Mr. Bullock, of Marlton, fills the pulpit just vacated by Mr. Lorenzo Appleby.

The Baptists are considering the matter of a Sabbath school entertainment for Christmas and the Methodists are practicing their school for the same purpose.

In casting about I find there are nine daily papers received here every day and a much larger number of weeklies.

E. J. Cook, our enterprising clothing dealer has a circulating library in his store that may yet grow to be one of the institutions of the place.

We have in our place three doctors, Stetson L. Bacon, Bewley and Henry C. Fithian, and one undertaker. Having but one undertaker is proof conclusion that our doctors are all ok.

Just now a goodly number of our oystermen are "tied up" while others are dredging the bay for the (at present) rather poor bivalve.

Captain Jacob Liber is, I understand, confined to the house from sickness.

Samuel Fagan's house is enclosed and nearly ready for the masons.

December 5

Mr. Samuel Meredith, the barber, can stand a great deal but the present stand is too cold for him and consequently he is about to vacate it. "Bucky" is a good barber and deserving patronage.

Mr. Samuel Porter moved yesterday to Mr. John Garrison's house on Railroad Avenue.

Captain Hinson was very sea sick last Monday so he could not eat any dinner, and he could not eat any dinner, and he said "My how I wish I was home" but by the medical aid of his crew he soon recovered, but was wishing he was home all the time.

Mr. William Chew has a game rooster which he challenges the place for a prize fight.

Mr. Daniel Robbins has a nice double house raised and nearly enclosed, on corner of Washington and Brown streets. We understand it is for rent. There are also more empty houses and parts of houses for rent here.

Cool weather will make markets better for oysters.

December 7

Captain Andrew Vail, of schooner "Elvina English," has a very nice suit of sails, made by James Mulvey.

Captain Andy McFarland, of Philadelphia, employed by Robert W. DuBois, sail maker, is going to return home the last of this week.

Walter Peterson is building a very pretty house on Mauricetown road.

Schooner "Caroline," loaded with oysters, on Wednesday night last during the gale struck on East Point Bar and sunk. She has since been raised and lying at the wharf all night.

Mr. Samuel L. Meredith, barber of Long Reach, is going to close out his business and locate elsewhere. Sam will be greatly missed by his friends.

Mr. and Mrs. George Young left Monday for Cape May.

The schooner "S. C. Kimble," Captain Henry Lake, arrived at the wharf at Long Reach Saturday. The sails were one solid sheet of ice.

Miss Lizzie Hand, daughter of Warrington L. Hand, has returned home after visiting friends in Clarksboro and Philadelphia.

Mr. John Williams has rented the house now occupied by Mr. Wallie Stites as the latter is to where Theodore Fleetwood now lives.

December 8

Oysterman say they suffered more from the cold, coming down from Philadelphia on Thursday last, than for many a year. It has been so cold lately that the oyster boats in Maurice River cove have not been able to go out to work. Oystermen dread this kind of weather and cannot work. Oysters freeze as soon as caught.

December 9

Mr. William Bloxsom and family moved from South Church Street to Middletown in part of Mrs. Mahaley Compton's house and Mrs. Elizabeth Whitaker of Newport is to move where the former vacated.

Mr. Theodore Fleetwood, principal of school, has rented one half of Captain Henry's house, where Samuel Porter left.

A good many are enjoying this snow by sleighing, as the bells are tingling most of the time. They say it is first rate sleighing.

Oyster markets are good now.

December 11

Mr. Lewis Andrews and wife have gone to Philadelphia to spend the winter.

Mr. Samuel Lake, Jr., is a happy man. It's a girl!

Mrs. Heritage and Mrs. Cox were in Bridgeton Thursday, and Mrs. David T. Robbins in Philadelphia.

December 15

Mrs. Samuel Shinn, of Port Norris, was given a pleasant surprise party recently by a number of her friends from Millville, Vineland, Haleyville and other places dropping in on her to celebrate her birthday. All enjoyed themselves hugely and before they left presented Mrs. Shinn with a pair of gold spectacles.

John Moore, of the firm of Moore & Reeves, Port Norris, has been spending a few days in this city.

Mrs. Theodore Fleetwood and Wallie Stites have both moved.

Mrs. Elizabeth Whitaker, of Newport, has moved here to-day on, South Church street.

Mr. Hugh H. Nickerson has a splendid line of furniture and it is very cheap.

David T. Robbins has a big lot of Christmas goods. Almost everything you can mention for sale is there.

Both churches are practicing for Christmas exercises.

Reverend Mr. Rumphy, of Philadelphia, will preach in the Baptist church next Sunday.

December 16

At Port Norris Mr. Theodore Fleetwood, the school teacher has moved into a new house, and Wallie Stites occupies the place he has just vacated.

Today Mrs. Elizabeth Whitaker, of Newport is moving into one of Mr. John English's houses.

Charles Whitaker came home very sick last night, from off the sloop "Maud M. Robbins."

There is not much news at the Port just now.

December 19

Saturday evening there was a masquerade party at Captain George Webb's residence. It was quite a surprise for the Captain, as he was totally in the dark as to the matter. About thirty persons were present, and they had a good time.

The sloop "Trader" has not yet been heard from, and there are grave fears as to whether both vessel and crew haven't been lost.

Mr. S. Gland's trotting horse has proved very smart. He offers to bet that the animal will go a mile in 2.14, and he values it at $1,850.

Reverend J. R. Thompson, of the Methodist Episcopal Church, commenced a series of illustrated sermons at yesterday's service. They are very interesting.

Sutton and Haines are selling first class beef steak, and many people say they are the most enterprising butchers we have ever had at the Port.

Sunday morning and evening, the Reverend W. W. Bullock, of Marlton, Camden County preached in the Baptist Church. His text in the morning was from 1st Peter, 1st chapter, and part of the 13th verse: "*Wherefore gird up the loins of your mind*." In the evening the text was from 1st Peter, 2nd chapter, 6th verse: "***Behold I lay in Zion a chief corner stone, elect, precious; and that believeth on him shall not be confounded.***" Mr. Bullock is a fine speaker, and both sermons were excellent.

"Dickie" Compton is an old, experienced hand in the painting business. He served his apprenticeship with his father, T.G. Compton, for twenty-one years, and has since been contracting for a period so long, he says, that his memory runneth not to the contrary.

Captain Henry S. Robbins informs us that the vessel, launched not long since, of which he owns a share, is named "Isaac T. Nichols," of which name he is proud." *Port Norris Gazette*

December 22

Mrs. George Everingham and children have gone to Cape May to spend Christmas.

Mrs. Samuel Parsons and children have also gone away to spend the holidays.

Mr. Daniel Robbins has been making use of what good weather we have just had to have his new house painted.

The Baptists have a different preacher in their pulpit nearly every Sunday now. Mr. Humphrey, last Sunday, was very much liked, and is to come again next Saturday week. Next Sunday Reverend Mr. Alvin will preach for them.

December 23

The Methodists are to have their Christmas entertainment on Friday evening. All over fourteen years are to pay ten cents to go towards buying the children presents. The Baptist entertainment will take place on the same night. It is free. Everybody be sure and come get your presents and hear the speaking, dialogues, singing, &c, and don't forget to have a present put in for your friends. News is scarce and mud is plentiful.

There was sort of a bread famine in Port Norris yesterday. The baker there went to Philadelphia to spend Christmas and did not show up, but it's "an ill wind that blows no good" so Hughes, the baker in this city, got an order for one hundred loaves to go to Port Norris.

Port Norris Entertainment

Perhaps the best entertainment ever given by the Baptist Sunday school, of Port Norris, was that of Christmas Eve, under the direction of Miss Lizzie Bacon. The entire programme was rendered in excellent taste and exhibited talent quite equal to the best we have seen in much larger places. The music in charge of Mrs. Lee and Stites was exceptionally good toward the close of the exercises. Many valuable presents were distributed, among then a fine tenor horn, watches, valuable writing desks, and a large number of other beautiful and useful articles. Early in the evening it began to rain, and threatened for a time to interfere with arrangements, but the church was well filled and all were happy. We learn that our Methodist friends had a similar exhibition, and for a time we were concerned that it might be at the same time.

SCRIBBLER

December 24

An Outrage

One of the grossest abuses that is possible for any authorities to heap upon a man, was imposed upon Charles Harris, of Port Norris, on Saturday last, by the officers of the Vineland Bank and Constables Wells and Clark, of Millville .

On Saturday, a note for $159.00 drawn on Millville bank, signed by James Smith, of Dragstown, and indorsed by Isaac B. Mulford, was presented to the Vineland National Bank. The person presenting the note was a man about five feet high, sandy hair and smooth face. The man did not succeed in getting the note cashed, as the officials were somewhat suspicious. The signature was pronounced a forgery, and a warrant was issued for the arrest of Charles Harris, an employee of Ewing & Ware, Port Norris.

Armed with this warrant Constables Wells and Clark, of Vineland, proceeded to Port Norris where they arrested Harris. Mr. Harris does not answer the description of the man at all, as he stands about 6 feet high, dark hair and moustache. Before taking Harris from Port Norris the Constables told his wife and also hotel keeper S. Irwin Middleton that Harris was not the man wanted, but notwithstanding they drove him over to Vineland. When taken before the Vineland Bank officials they immediately announced that he was not the man wanted. Harris was then released and his fare paid to Millville, and from there he was compelled to walk to Port Norris in the drenching rain.

Mr. Harris is well known in Port Norris, and his friends are very indignant at the manner in which he was handled by the officers, and are loud in denunciation of their actions.

December 27

Mr. James Phillips was presented with another fine son recently.

Mr. David Turner moved from here to Dividing Creek.

Mr. William Parsons and family have moved up from Long Reach to Church and Main Streets.

A wedding took place here on Christmas.

Mrs. Sallie Bowen, of Dividing Creek is at her father's, Mr. Sloan's, to spend the holidays.

December 28

I suppose some of your readers don't know who it was that was married on Christmas so I will tell you, Mr. Stultz Roley of this place, and Miss Josephine Compton, of Mauricetown. They were married by Reverend J. R. Thompson. We are looking for several more weddings soon.

Reverend Brooks Robbins and friends are here visiting the former's mother and others.

Mr. Whitefield Thompson is the happy father and it's a girl.

Part of Reverend Mr. Corson's family are visiting the recent pastor of the Methodist Episcopal Church.

Mr. Alex Whitten, of Philadelphia, has been visiting mine host S. Irwin Middleton. On a gunning expedition they succeeded in bagging 40 pair of birds and a number of rabbits.

A shooting match took place here Saturday morning in which ten persons took part. The number of birds to each man was ten. The match was tied by C. Campbell and Samuel Ferguson, each man bringing down eight birds. In the afternoon to decide the tie birds were again put up. Mr. Ferguson shot and killed one, making nine dead birds. Mr. Campbell then shot at his bird and missed. This won the prize for Mr. Ferguson, which was a handsome double barreled gun valued at $50.

A. S. Nichelson, of Long Branch, is helping his brother, Hugh H. Nickelson, furniture dealer.

William Parsons has moved from Long Reach into part of Daniel Robbins house on Main Street.

Schooner "Gratitude," commanded by Captain Ellis Hand, one day last week while dredging in the cove sprung a leak and was compelled to run into Long Reach for repairs.

Mr. James Mulvey has just finished a very neat suit of sails for schooner "Lucy."

Edward Reeves, assistant agent at Port Norris, spent Christmas at home in Greenwich.

James Mulvey and Joseph Low went to Bridgeton Saturday afternoon to measure the new schooner of Mark Townsend for a suit of sails.

Mr. Grant Hodder and sister Anna are visiting Miss Jane Robbins.

Thomas P. Covington, of Philadelphia, has been visiting Robert H. Bloxsom.

Mr. J. C. Warner and wife, parents of Mrs. S. Irwin Middleton, spent Sunday here.

December 29

You need not be surprised if there are a lot of mistakes in the Port Norris "Gazette" this week, nor if George Magee should appear slightly absent minded.

Both churches had a fine time at Christmas. Lots of presents were read off besides one to every Sunday school attendant, scholars and teachers.

Our people are pleased to learn that the Knights got the organ. Big time to-night, Knights of Pythias.

Mr. Gilbert Compton, from Smalley's nursery, Roadstown, is in town taking orders for trees, vines and shrubbery.

Edward S. Reeves, of Harmony, paid his son a short visit.

Gunners report game is very scarce around this vicinity.

Prayer meeting in the Methodist Episcopal Church tonight at the usual hour.

There was only seven car loads of oysters shipped from Long Reach today. William B. Pepper shipped fifteen sacks of oysters to S.M. Ogden of Bridgeton.

Mr. Grant Hodder and his sister Anna returned to their home in the city.

Undertaker Hugh Nicholson had charge of the funeral of Miss Sallie Tullis of Dividing Creek.

William Bennett, who has been visiting at Captain Andrew Vail's, has returned home.

December 30

Big Sensation at Port Norris

CUMBERLAND CIRCUIT COURT

Leonard C. Hand}

Vs

Charles D. Lake}

Looks innocent don't it!

And yet thereby hangs a tale which is likely to shake Port Norris to its social centre, and the unfolding of which will make this one of the celebrated cases on Cumberland's Civil Calendar.

A few days ago Sheriff Williams visited Port Norris and served upon Captain Lake, a paper requiring him to "be and appear," etc.

The receipt of this document seemed to agitate the Captain considerably, and great curiosity has been manifested to know what was up. This morning the cat emerged from the bag.

Messrs. Reeves and Bacon, Attorneys for Captain Hand, filed in the County Clerk's Office, the declaration in the case setting forth the cause of action. It is a somewhat lengthy document replete with "whereases" and "to wits," but stripped of its legal verbiage and put into United States, is substantially as follows:

It begins by stating that Leonard C. Hand is a good, true, honest and faithful citizen of this State, that his reputation, especially for honesty, always been of the best in the community where he lives.

That Charles D. Lake well knowing these facts and greatly envying his happy state with guile in his heart and malice on his tongue, willfully and maliciously slandered him.

That on a certain day in the presence of diverse good and worthy citizens of this state and neighbors of the plaintiff, the said defendant falsely and maliciously, spake and published, of and concerning the said plaintiff the false, scandalous, malicious and defamatory words following, that is to say, Leonard Hand, (meaning they said plaintiff) is the chicken that stole my, (meaning his, the said defendant's) oysters, meaning thereby that the said plaintiff was a thief.

That by reason of this conversation some of these "good and worthy citizens" refuse to have their accustomed dealings with Captain Hand and he is thereby injured and damnified, and demands damages of a large amount.

Inquiry reveals the fact that Captain Hand is a young, energetic and enterprising citizen of Port Norris, an extensive planter of oysters, a man highly esteemed in the community. Why Captain Lake should charge this crime upon him is as yet an unsolved mystery. Captain Hand, strong in his consciousness of innocence seems determined to show his accuser, that if he is a "chicken" he is a specimen of the game variety.

Still another new baby in town. Mr. Willis Robbins is the happy father this time.

Mrs. John Sheldon and family are visiting Mr. Jesse ______ here.

Mr. Lorenzo Burnite is very poorly in health and has been for some time.

December 31

The *Salem Standard* announces that Charles Harris, of Port Norris, is in the county jail at Bridgeton for forging the name of J. B. Mulford to a check for $150. This comes from putting too much confidence in a not always correct morning paper of this city.

Warrington Snell, a boy aged about 13, had a very narrow escape from being drowned at Dividing Creek mill pond Wednesday while skating.

TULLIS – At Port Norris, December 28th, Sallie B. Tullis, aged 18 years.

ROBINSON – SHROPSHIRE – At Haleyville, December 25th, by Reverend George S. Senser, Samuel H. Robbins and Amanda Shropshire, both of Haleyville.

GLOSSARY

Apoplexy – meaning stroke, generally associated with paralysis.

Ancient Order – Knights of the Mystic Chain – The *Knights* of the *Ancient Order* of the *Mystic Chain* were a secret society in the US in the late nineteenth century. Founded by Freemasons in 1871, the group had a strong Masonic influence in its rituals and degrees, as well as incorporating elements from the Bible and Arthurian legend.

Bi – old term meaning bicycle.

Consumption – Tuberculosis, a wasting sickness, cancer.

Esquire – a very old English word that was a title of dignity or rank. In early America it referred to a person holding a title of an office. Examples would include Politicians, Sheriffs, Justice of the Peace, etc.

Freshet - the flood of a river from heavy rain or melted snow; a rush of fresh water flowing into the sea.

Long Reach – early name for Bivalve, located just below Port Norris.

Millinery – trade or business of a milliner, women's hats.

Odd Fellows – Evolving from the Order of Odd Fellows first founded in England during the 1700s, the Independent Order of Odd Fellows (IOOF) is a non-political and non-sectarian international fraternal order founded in 1819 by Thomas Wildey in Baltimore, Maryland.

Oyster City – Nickname given to Port Norris due to the immense amount of oysters that passed through the town.

Pleurisy - inflammation of the pleurae, which impairs their lubricating function and causes pain when breathing. It is caused by pneumonia and other diseases of the chest or abdomen.

Pugilistic – a person who fights with the fists; a boxer, usually a professional.

Red Men –The Improved Order of Red Men is a fraternal order established in 1834. Their rituals and regalia are modeled after those assumed to be used by Native Americans. The organization claimed a membership of about half a million in 1935, but has declined to a little more than 15,000.

Rheumatism - any disease marked by inflammation and pain in the joints, muscles, or fibrous tissue, especially rheumatoid arthritis.

Set-to – A fight, brawl.

Typhoid Fever - an infectious bacterial fever with an eruption of red spots on the chest and abdomen and severe intestinal irritation.

Urbanity - suavity, courteousness, and refinement of manner.

Vendue - a public auction.

Welkin – The sky or heaven.

About the Index:

I have taken the liberty to change any page that had only a last name showing in the articles to include the first name, if known.

The changes have been verified by previous editions of this series or by consulting the available State and Federal Censuses.

Of course, as with any, work of this age, the reader should make their own determination of its accuracy.

INDEX

INDEX

INDEX